LOVE

THE

WORK

YOU'RE

WITH

LOVE
THE
WORK
YOU'RE
WITH

Find the Job You Always Wanted Without Leaving the One You Have

Richard C. Whiteley

HENRY HOLT AND COMPANY

NEW YORK

Henry Holt and Company, LLC
Publishers since 1866
115 West 18th Street
New York, New York 10011
Henry Holt® is a registered trademark of Henry Holt and Company, LLC.

"How to Overcome Your Strengths" reprinted from the May 1999 issue of *Fast Company* magazine. All rights reserved. To subscribe, call 800-542-6029 or visit www.fastcompany.com.

Patch Adams, copyright © 2001 by Universal City Studios, Inc. Courtesy of Universal Publishing Rights, a division of Universal Studios, Inc. All rights reserved.

The Life Orientation Test, copyright © 1994 by the American Psychological Association. Adapted with permission.

The Success-Fearing Personality, copyright © 1996 by Donnah Canavan, Katherine Garner, and Peter Gumpert. Adapted with permission.

Library of Congress Cataloging-in-Publication Data
Whiteley, Richard C.
    Love the work you're with: find the job you always wanted without leaving the one you have / Richard C. Whiteley. — 1st ed.
        p. cm.
    Includes bibliographical references and index.
    ISBN 0-8050-6592-X (hb)
    1. Job satisfaction. 2. Job enrichment. 3. Success in business. 4. Attitude (Psychology)
5. Motivation (Psychology) I. Title.

HF5549.5.J63 W484 2001
650.1'3—dc21   00-046196

Henry Holt books are available for special promotions and premiums. For details contact:
Director, Special Markets.
First Edition 2001
Designed by Jo Anne Metsch

Printed in the United States of America
1   3   5   7   9   10   8   6   4   2

In loving memory of
Harold and Elizabeth Whiteley
who started me on this amazing
journey called life

Contents

LOVE

THE

WORK

YOU'RE

WITH

Welcome . . .

I WAS ENJOYING THE game for two reasons. First, it was darn good hockey. Second, my beloved Bruins were skating their archrival, the Montreal Canadiens, off the ice, a rarity in those days.

There I was, totally absorbed when, *whoosh,* a bright blur of blue and yellow flashed in the corner of my eye. The blue was the uniform of Dave Kerpen, a vendor at Boston's Fleet Center, and the yellow was the box of Crunch 'n Munch he hurled to the guy three seats away.

While Fleet Center regulars around me smiled knowingly, I was astounded, as Dave, known more familiarly as "The Crunch 'n Munch Man," began to dance and jump wildly to the sonic booming of the rock music blasting out of the arena's loud speakers. Sometimes he would hold one yellow box aloft and swivel his hips in a manner Elvis would have envied. At other times, he would clap two boxes together with an exaggerated arm motion in perfect synchronization to the driving beat. The Crunch 'n Munch man was in full form. The more he got into his routine, the more fans from all over the stadium loved it. In fact, Dave's antics are regularly displayed on the huge TV monitor that hangs over center ice.

Dave was able to throw the yellow boxes to waiting patrons as many as six or seven rows away, hitting his target with the accuracy of a Super Bowl quarterback. What followed this physical tour de force amazed me. I noticed that one buyer, after "receiving" his Crunch 'n Munch, threw it right back to Dave. I was puzzled. Were they playing catch? Did the guy change his mind and opt for the ice-cream sandwich instead? No! He threw it back so he could—get this—have Dave autograph it! Dave signed the box with a large felt pen he had at the ready and heaved it back.

The net result was that everyone in the area, whether they went for the Crunch 'n Munch or not, had a great time. Dave was obviously in his glory and he moved a lot of Crunch 'n Munch—*a lot*. Since having been assigned this notoriously slow-moving product to hawk in the aisles, he has increased sales a whopping 400 percent![1]

If Dave confined himself to his job description he would be no more than your average peanut vendor sauntering up and down the aisles, box of goodies raised, yelling "Hey, get your Crunch 'n Munch here!" But no. He turned a routine sales job into high-flying, first-class entertainment, and in the process took arena vending to new heights of productivity and value.

"So what," you may ask, "does this have to do with me? I'm not a peanut vendor." Well, if Dave Kerpen proves one thing, it is this: there is no such thing as a boring job. If he can create positive results out of his challenging work circumstances, there's no telling what you might be able to do with yours.

When I hear someone complaining about the drudgery of his or her job, I think of Dave and other happy workers I've seen or heard about: the singing bus driver; the flight attendant who makes announcements in a Donald Duck voice; the wildly successful baker who "falls in love with the dough" each morning; and "Dr. Shine," who dedicates his life to helping people feel good about themselves from the shoes up. You may not know these people, but you certainly know others like them. They are the workers who turn the ordinary into the magical, the mundane into the magnificent.

Selling Crunch 'n Munch may not be Dave Kerpen's ultimate dream job—he graduated from Boston University with a double major—but because he infuses it with "dream job" spirit, it delivers great rewards. It is meaningful because he makes others happy. It gives him recognition because only he can do what he does in the way he does it. It makes him productive. And obviously, it brings him great joy.

Whether you're a peanut vendor, or a middle manager, or the CEO of a global empire, each of us has the freedom to infuse passion and spirit into whatever it is we are doing at this very moment. Why? Because *jobs don't have spirit . . . people do.* Like Dave Kerpen, we can break out of self-imposed or externally implied expectations, figure out ways to snap open our passion, and then pour it into whatever it is we do. When that happens, the job we have will start to seem like the job we've always wanted. Ultimately, it's our spirit that delivers "dream job" rewards—meaning, recognition, productivity, and joy.

For some of you, infusing spirit into your current job may seem impossible. If so, then perhaps it is time to make a change. But before you call a headhunter, consider the old adage: "The more things change the more they stay the same." How often have you seen a person switch jobs only to find the same problems repeating themselves at the new one? Or how about changing relationships? How many people do you know who leave one person only to find the same issues appearing again with another? At some point it isn't about changing jobs or partners, it's about changing ourselves. We get stuck in our own unconscious patterns of attitude and behavior and, unable to see them, blame our circumstances rather than ourselves for causing the problems. And when we do change we simply take these invisible patterns into the new situation where they strike again.

Love the Work You're With will give you the opportunity to identify some of those patterns and, if you are tempted to quit your job, challenge you to check the patterns first. When you do, you just might find the job you always wanted without having to leave the one you already have. And if you don't? You will be able to move on without dragging along those bothersome patterns that will prevent you from flourishing in your new situation. The underlying idea is, first try to find passion in your work and then, if that doesn't work, find work you are passionate about.

There are many unanticipated "external factors" that affect your happiness at work. A layoff, a merger, missing a bonus, a product failure, an insensitive manager. Such unwelcome surprises will always be a component of your work. They are unpredictable and ubiquitous. Because of the infinite variety and number of such intrusions, there are simply not enough pages for us to deal with such specific counsel. Rather our focus will be on the "internal factors"—the attitudes, knowledge, and skills—that you bring to your work situation and how you can use them to cope with and even capitalize on such external disruptions.

There is an old saying: "Give a man a fish and he eats for a day. Teach a man to fish and he eats for a lifetime." The intent of this book is to teach you how to "fish" by developing those internal resources that will help you find more joy and productivity in your work, no matter what is happening around you.

Time and time again, people who make the internal changes that allow them to love the work they're with find that all of a sudden work isn't work any longer. Rather it is transformed into a state where all parts of them—hands, head, heart, and spirit—are fully engaged. They don't check their private persona at the company's front door and put on a public one. They work as whole people—people without fear of reprisals for having a sense of humor, for having faults, for pushing the boundaries of what is expected.

Businesses have done much to discourage the expression of individual spirit. They have reengineered, downsized, merged, and acquired. They've increased workloads, decreased budgets, and all too often rolled out a high-sounding set of visions and values conspicuously absent in the behavior of senior management. While researching my last book, *Customer-Centered Growth*, we talked to more than two hundred companies on six continents. What do you think was the one word most often used to describe company culture? *Fearful.*

Obviously, with fear so pervasive, people's productivity and enjoyment of their work have suffered greatly. And that is why I have written this book—to help you locate that engaging, ebullient spirit that lives in you, that lives in each of us.

So what about you, your spirit, and your work? Where are you? To find out, try answering the six questions below:

1. Does your work create energy rather than drain it?
2. When work pressures increase, are you able to remain calm, grounded, and clear?
3. Are you able to find the positives in negative situations at work?
4. When *you* are the obstacle to getting what you want, are you able to see it and fix it?
5. Have you enlisted the support of specific individuals who can help you get what you want at work?
6. Are you able to be yourself at work, rather than who you think others want you to be?

If you have answered "No" to any of the above, and would have preferred a "Yes," then this book can help you make improvements. It describes six ways of being: *Follow Your Passion, Be Home, Create Your Own Reality, Get Out of Your Own Way, Foster Your Interdependence,* and *Be Yourself*—each of which corresponds to one of the questions above. Though there are many ways of being that may be useful, these six are offered as a starting point. They have greatly enriched my life and my work with hundreds of organizations and thousands of business-people. When they are in action, good things happen.

- In "Follow Your Passion" (chapter 1), you will learn how to increase your passion for your work, wed your work to a purpose, and reengineer your job for greater joy and productivity.

- In "Be Home" (chapter 2), you will learn how to access that place inside you that brings out the best in you as a performer and enables you to face trials at work with rock-solid groundedness.

- In "Create Your Own Reality" (chapter 3), you will learn how to use optimism at work to your advantage—mining positive results

from setbacks and creating a "career story" that helps you attain what
you want in your work life.

- In "Get Out of Your Own Way" (chapter 4), you will look at how
you typically stop yourself at work and how to bring and develop
your own genius in your work.

- In "Foster Your Interdependence" (chapter 5), you will focus on
getting connected at work, and identifying and assembling your perfect Personal Board of Directors.

- In "Be Yourself" (chapter 6), you will learn why speaking frankly,
lightening up, and being your own best ally is essential to a spirited
work life.

- Finally, "Leader's Guide: How to Create a Spirited Workforce"
(chapter 7) is devoted to those of you who lead teams and want to
create a work climate that will bring greater happiness *and* productivity to your employees. In addition, a leadership self-assessment
questionnaire is included as an appendix if you wish to evaluate
your strengths and areas for improvement as a leader.

I have learned that change must be self-directed. It simply can't be
imposed from the outside. To make this book work for you, I would
reinforce this thought. The success you gain from *Love the Work You're
With* is up to you and based on what you actually do—not think about
doing, but *do*.

To assist you, each chapter offers a variety of assessment tools and
exercises specially designed to help guide your thinking, and your soul,
about the big questions—what are my goals, what brings me happiness,
what makes me perform at my best? They are meant to enable you to
assess where you are and to begin applying the concepts to your unique
work situation immediately.

I've gone through this process myself after years on a traditional job
track, and what I've found is that when all is said and done there are
but five "Action Steps" you can take to promote change. You can either

do *more* of something, do *less, start, stop,* and/or do it *differently.* The Start, Stop, More, Less, Differently decision-making framework will be presented at the end of each chapter under the heading, "Action Steps," to help you convert the insight you will gain from each chapter into specific, job-enhancing actions.

There are no "musts," "shoulds," or "got to's"—no guilt trips in this book. For me to tell you what you "should" do would be presumptuous. Rather, reading this book represents an opportunity to step back and take a look at one of the most important areas of your existence, your work life, and make some changes if you choose.

I believe that for a book like this to be helpful a kind of trust must be established between you, the reader, and me, the author. With this in mind, let me share some of myself beyond what you might have read on the jacket cover. My intent is clear. I have dedicated my life to being in service to others, and my life purpose is to help bring spirit back into work. My wish is that the ideas contained in this book make as profound a difference in your life as they have mine.

After college I served aboard a minesweeper in the U.S. Navy, where I learned about human nature and leadership. Later I got an M.B.A., went into business, and shortly thereafter started my own company with several colleagues. In the last thirty years, we have seen our company grow into a 700-person global training and consulting firm. I have had the privilege of getting to know and serve more than 300 different organizations in many different industries and public sectors. I have also had the privilege of speaking before 150,000 businesspeople in more than twenty-six countries.

Like most people, I've had personal struggles that affected my work life, whether or not I acknowledged them at the time—or even told my colleagues. Some of these challenges—early learning disabilities, the death of both parents within five months, and a painful divorce—forced me to look more closely at my choices in both life and work. As a result of some of these life issues I have spent the past twenty years focusing on my personal as well as professional growth.

So do I consider myself the perfect role model for the Six Ways of

Being? Not at all. For me it is not a question of always being able to embody these approaches. The key is to know where you want to be, notice when you are not there, and get back on track. Mastery of the Six Ways of Being is having this awareness and, over time, being on track an increasing percentage of the time. This is the spirit of this book. It is not about perfection, it is about process.

In order to give you a more precise indication of the extent to which you love the work you're with, I invite you to complete the self-assessment questionnaire that follows this "Welcome." It has been designed to help you get the most out of this book. Like many self-assessments, it helps you identify the areas where you have the greatest need or opportunity for improvement. I hope you will take some time to think about yourself and your work as you consider each question; your candid answers will point you directly to the chapters that will be of most use to you. The point is, let this book work for you in the way that is best for you. If you care to share your experiences with or reactions to this book, I would love to hear them. You will find my address at the end of the book or you can reach me through my Web site: www.whiteleygroup.com.

Perhaps the best way to summarize what I have said above is to share a poem with you. John Foucher gave it to my wife, Sharon, and me upon his graduation from the Carroll School, a wonderful place for children with learning difficulties. We established the Sunrise Foundation to fully sponsor one student, from acceptance through graduation. In fact, a percentage of the proceeds of this book will be used to fund this important tradition. John was Sunrise's first graduate and, on that momentous day, he gave us a gift. It was a framed copy of a poem he found in his great-grandfather's chest after he passed away. The poem:

One ship goes East, another West
By the selfsame winds that blow
'Tis the set of the sail and not the gale
That determine the way they go.

Like the ships at sea, are the ways of fate
As we voyage along through life
'Tis the set of the soul that decides the goal
And not the calm or strife

— ELLA WHEELER COX

I hope this book will make a difference for you.

Richard Whiteley

LOVE THE WORK YOU'RE WITH
SELF-ASSESSMENT

THIS SELF-ASSESSMENT has been designed to help you get the most out of *Love the Work You're With*. By completing it you can decide the extent to which you and your work can benefit from some fine-tuning. In addition you will be able to identify those areas that have the greatest need for improvement and then go directly to the chapter(s) that will be of the most immediate help to you.

For best results respond to each statement with total candor. As with the other exercises in this book your responses need only be known to you. If you are concerned about someone seeing your answers consider photocopying the self-assessment exercise and completing it outside of this book.

This self-assessment process is intended to help you as you go about improving your work situation. The numbers are only guidelines. Use your own judgment about what will work best for you.

DIRECTIONS

Place the number that best describes you next to each statement below:

4 = Always
3 = Usually
2 = Sometimes
1 = Seldom
0 = Never

A.

_____ 1. My work creates passion in me rather than draining it.

_____ 2. I know my life's purpose.

_____ 3. I have a positive attitude about my job.

_____ *Total*

B.

_____ 4. When work pressures increase I am able to remain calm, grounded, and clear.

_____ 5. When work pressures increase I am able to stay in the present.

_____ 6. I don't become obsessed with goals and performance targets.

_____ *Total*

C.

_____ 7. Even when things are going very wrong, I can find the positives in the situation.

_____ 8. I use adversity as a teacher to improve future performance.

___ 9. No matter what has happened in my life to date, I view it as a positive contributor to my work.

___ *Total*

D.

___10. When I am the obstacle between me and what I want at work, I am able to see that and fix it.

___11. At work I use mistakes to create a positive result.

___12. I have unique talents or knowledge that make me special at work.

___ *Total*

E.

___13. I am purposeful in staying connected to people at work who can help me to do my job well.

___14. I have a specific group of people who act as my advisors when I am considering work-related issues.

___15. I have formally asked people who can help me with work-related matters to be my advisor.

___ *Total*

F.

___16. At work I am comfortable telling the truth.

___17. I have great compassion for myself when I make major mistakes at work.

___18. When things are going badly at work, I am able to lighten up and find the humor in tough situations.

___ *Total*

Grand total of A–F ___

Interpreting Your Self-Assessment

YOUR GRAND TOTAL is an indication of the extent you are able to *Love the Work You're With*. The lowest possible score is 0 and the highest is 72. Where do you stand in comparison to the guidelines below?

0–14	It appears that you derive little joy from your work. What keeps you from bringing all of you to work? How can you change it? Who is someone you trust who can offer helpful perspectives and advice?
15–28	It appears that you are not fully comfortable bringing all of you to work. What gets in the way? How can you change it? Select one way of being and plan to make it a strength. Who is someone you trust who can offer helpful perspectives and advice?
29–42	There are some strengths to build upon. Continue to use them. Which way of being would have the greatest positive impact if developed? Who can be of help to you?
43–57	You appear to be getting a lot out of your work. Use the strong practices to support your efforts. Select one or two activities to improve, and develop a plan to do so.
58–72	You appear to have a good match with your job. Fine-tuning is appropriate. Continue doing what works. Select one or two activities to improve, and develop a plan to do so.

Interpreting the Six Ways of Being

REVIEW THE SIX total scores you placed next to A, B, C, D, E, and F. The lowest score indicates a priority for improvement. If your lowest score was:

A	then start with chapter	1
B	then start with chapter	2
C	then start with chapter	3
D	then start with chapter	4
E	then start with chapter	5
F	then start with chapter	6

Interpreting Individual Scores

WHICH OF THE eighteen statements has your lowest score? This is the highest priority area for your focus and improvement efforts.

My greatest area for improvement is: _____.

Follow Your Passion

If you love something, you'll bring so much of yourself to it that it will create your future.

— FRANCIS FORD COPPOLA[1]

FOR A SOLID week in 1976 the owner of Boston's newest hot-concept furniture retailer, George Hamilton of Hamilton's, tried to eat in peace. Not easy. Not with the constant droning of that airplane circling outside. What kind of insanity possessed that woman to spend thousands of dollars to buzz Hamilton's building daily during lunch towing a sign that read "Hire Judy George . . . She'll Make You Millions!"?

The plane-hirer was Judy George, founder and now chairperson and CEO of the upscale furniture chain, Domain, and the author of *The Intuitive Businesswoman* and *The Domain Book of Intuitive Home Design*.

What Hamilton mistook for "insanity" was passion.

Years earlier, while other young girls were tearing out magazine pictures of their idols and taping them to their bedroom walls, Judy George was putting up pictures of rooms.[2] While other kids spent a summer's day setting up a lemonade stand, Judy opened a chain of them — twenty to thirty — in front of the factories that lined the downtown of her hometown Everett, Massachusetts. She staffed her stands with kids from the neighborhood whom she employed to help her to raise the $16 she needed for a community-sponsored boat trip.

Need Your Job

STILL — DESPITE SUCH early entrepreneurial signals — the day that Judy told her husband and father of her four children that she wanted to start her own business, he fell off the couch, literally. "He couldn't understand. What more could I want? We were financially stable and certainly I had enough to do with taking care of the children. But as an entrepreneur he did understand 'need.' I'm not spiritual in the traditional sense, but there was something bigger guiding me to do this thing that I just couldn't ignore. I *needed* to do it. That he understood."

Judy's first business, "Ideas by George," which sold her marketing ideas and promoted her decorating skills via television interviews and a newspaper column, was fun, but, in Judy's words, "didn't make any money." Then Hamilton's came to town. "I saw this ad about a new concept starting up," she says. "I sent in a great résumé, TV tapes, letters. George Hamilton said that although I was a 'star,' that didn't prove anything." In spite of her track record, Hamilton refused her an interview. "So, I secretly borrowed $10,000 from my husband's bank account and hired a plane," she says. Hamilton had her served by the police with a cease-and-desist order. Then he hired her.

Over time, Hamilton's became Scandinavian Designs and Judy became its president. She eventually left and opened Domain with three investors and a boatload of passion. Today, Domain is a 23-store chain that grosses $60 million a year. So just what was this "need" Judy felt and where did it come from?

Judy's Passion: *There's No Place Like Home*

JUDY HAS HAD a chance to reflect on what drove that little girl with chutzpah and a penchant for lemonade stands and beautiful rooms to such achievement. She traces the roots of that entrepreneurial passion for home furnishings to her childhood.

"I remember watching *The Wizard of Oz* and there was Dorothy desperately trying to get back home. I was crushed. I knew just how she felt. *Home*. To me that word is still so emotionally charged. My parents, whom I idolized, were working-class entrepreneurs and had no money. I remember watching out the window of my neighbor-caretaker's home as my father and mother left to go to work, taking my older sister with them. I must have been about three years old, too young to go along. Somewhere deep inside I felt that I needed to do something to make them stay home with me. That's all I wanted and I wanted it desperately. Maybe if I achieved something they wouldn't leave me anymore. That's why as a kid I danced like mad—ballet, tap, you name it—just as a way to get them to recognize me. Onstage, I was screaming with my feet: 'Here I am! Stay! I'm worth it!' "

Judy's "need"—the source of her passion—was rooted in her notion of the picture-perfect home life her parents were unable to afford in the early years. "There is nothing glitzy or contemporary about Domain furnishings. It is all about nostalgia," says Judy, "about creating a warm, comfortable home." Ultimately Judy's parents' willingness to take risks as entrepreneurs and hard work paid off and they became successful. Those values were the wind beneath Judy's wings as she satisfied that need, that passion, to find her way to the idolized home she had longed for as a child. How appropriate that she chose the name Domain, the romance-language version of "home."

How Passion Leads to Extraordinary Achievement

JUDY WAS ABSOLUTELY compelled to become an entrepreneur by an internal need, a need so intrinsically excitable to her core, that it wouldn't let her rest until she found an outlet for its expression. That same infatuation and zeal—as opposed to blind ambition—that fueled Judy's dogged determination has been the impetus behind the success of a great many other businesspeople as well. Take Howard Schultz, CEO of Starbucks, for example.

In an episode of the television show *The Simpsons*, Homer Simpson walks into a shopping mall only to discover that every single store is a Starbucks—all but one, which has the words "Starbucks Coming Soon" emblazoned across it. Homer wasn't all that far off. Every day, some-where in the world, another Starbucks opens.

How did Schultz take this second-most-traded commodity in the world, coffee, and turn it into a global brand? Simply put, Schultz—in the words of a senior writer at *Fortune* magazine—is "extremely pas-sionate about coffee."[3]

While on a business trip to Italy, Schultz meandered into an espresso bar and had an epiphany. Why couldn't he import that coffee culture—the romance, the intense love of coffee, the social experience of the local espresso bar, the celebratory "taking a break" attitude—to America? He approached his bosses at Starbucks, who owned five tiny shops in Seattle at the time. They balked. Schultz parted company, opened his own espresso bar, and made enough money to eventually buy out his previous employers. The rest is history.

At the root of Starbucks's extraordinary success is the simple but pow-erful passion Schultz has for coffee, a passion that finds its way into the people who work for Starbucks, which then finds its way to customers. Much of Starbucks's success is directly attributed to its employees, who are classically trained as *barristas*—the espresso-bar equivalent of bartenders—and who Schultz deems more important than customers.

Schultz's father, a cabbie embittered by the way he was treated dur-ing his career, taught him the importance of dignity and respect for employees. Schultz has put his money where that passion is and is one of the few major users of part-time employees who provides medical insurance and other perks usually reserved for full-time workers. His allegiance to his workers is evidenced in myriad ways, including donating the entire ongoing profits from one store to fight violence after employees there were killed. One result of this people passion is an incredible retention rate of part-timers that not only startles other retailers but is also a prime factor in Starbucks's profitability.

Before Schultz's Starbucks, a cup of coffee was, well, just a cup of joe. Now there is an entire legion of coffee aficionados as well versed on beans and brewing methods as the most dedicated wine connoisseurs are on grapes and fermentation processes. Today Starbucks stands not only as an icon of the power of passion for a product but as the power of passion for the people who work there.

Schultz was lucky. His passion hit him like lightning. Judy was lucky. As a child, her passion implanted itself as an unquenched desire that simply had to be satisfied. Neither of them went looking for their "thing." Most of the rest of us, however, aren't so lucky. We need to look for our passion as though we are mining for gold. We need to go deep, think deep, and dig past preconceived limitations—what we think we are *supposed* to want to be versus what we *truly* want to be. By identifying the people and professions you admire, and the qualities you admire in both, you can discover the core characteristics of your own unique aspirations and values.

It is easy to fall into a trap of gravitating to those you think you *should* admire—today's business icons or yesterday's historical leaders, for example. Push yourself to unearth traits worth emulating in unlikely places. Tony LePore—who makes my list—is a great example of finding passion in an unlikely place.

When LePore directs traffic at a four-way intersection in downtown Providence, Rhode Island, he draws a crowd. Make that an audience. This is Oscar stuff. Passersby are stunned by his Nureyev spins and pirouettes, Michael Jackson gyrations, rhythmic whistle blowing and whirling arms that direct traffic this way and that with the utmost efficiency and logic.[4] LePore is on my most admired list because he transforms an ordinary job into a memorable and joyful experience for drivers, passersby, and most important for himself. He does it—right where he is, in the job he has now—through passion. Although I am not a Tony LePore—my personality is different, my job is different—whenever I start moping about the dullness of a particular aspect of my job, I think about him, about how his unique brand of passion transformed similarly mundane work, and I am immediately lifted out of my doldrums and into the world of possibility.

Uncover the Passion: *Start with What You Admire*

BEAUTIFUL ROOMS MOVED Judy George. A passion for coffee and disaffected workers moved Howard Schultz. What moves you? Looking at people you admire, careers you admire, and personal or professional characteristics you admire, can give you a vantage point to begin uncovering your own passion. Try this:

1. On a piece of paper make three columns with the headings: Individual/Profession/Characteristics. In the *Individual* column, list at least five people you admire greatly and would like to emulate. The more names and types of people you can list the better. Think of friends; family; acquaintances; fictional characters; businesspeople; political, spiritual, and academic leaders; artists; teachers; scientists; philosophers; and children. Get the idea?

2. Next to each name, list each individual's particular *Profession*.

3. In the *Characteristics* column, list the personal characteristics and attributes of their profession that you most admire.

4. Now review your list. Are there any people on it you feel you "should" admire because, perhaps, the person is an impressive public figure or someone your parents admired, rather than a true hero in your

own eyes? If so, substitute someone for whom you have heartfelt admiration.

Note the people and characteristics you chose and set aside this list for later.

Author and professional speaker Barbara Glanz says, "Make your job a masterpiece and sign your name to it." The opportunity in this chapter is to discover *your* passion at work, and sign your name to it. For many, the following three steps will go a long way to helping you do this:

1. Uncover your passion.
2. Discover your purpose.
3. Reengineer your job.

With these three activities, you can start to transform even the dreariest job into an enjoyable, productive, and pleasant work life.

UNCOVER YOUR PASSION

> *What is it the person cares about? What is it that matters? What does the person have genuine, spontaneous, unrehearsed, unmodulated, and unhomogenized energy for? What is at the core of the person's being?*
>
> —PETER B. VAILL,
> *Appreciative Management and Leadership*[5]

OF COURSE, BEFORE you can follow your passion you need to uncover it. What do we mean, exactly, when we talk about passion for your work? Passion is intense energy or emotion, good or bad. It is love in all its glorious forms of joy, glee, confidence, and serendipity.

Or hate with its ignoble spin-offs of jealousy, rage, and fear. When we talk about uncovering passion at work, we are talking about something more than motivation. For example, what parts of your job would you want to keep doing even if you weren't being paid? What parts would you be reluctant to leave behind if you were promoted? Or, if you listed all the elements of your job from most exciting and enjoyable to the least enjoyable, what would be at the top of the list? Right there at the top is where your passion, and your best potential for great work, lies. For some computer programmers, that top-of-the-list passion has led to greatness in the form of the revolutionary Linux operating system.

Understanding open source software is difficult for the multitudes of us who don't understand the difference between "config.sys" and "autoexec.bat." But for those who do, the programmers who write the code that makes computers work for us, open source software is an absolute gas. It is a new language that is owned by no one and is continually refined, debugged, and modified by volunteer programmers the world over, simply because it's fun.

These programmers, who get paid good money for their day jobs come home at night and do it again for free—for the sheer pleasure of it. To paraphrase renowned sculptor and painter Alberto Giacometti, they no longer work for anything tangible except the sensation they have while working. That's passion. The result? Great works of art. While for Giacometti it is literally great artwork, for businesspeople, it's artistry as displayed through innovations, breakthroughs, zero defects, and exceeded targets. The kind of results any of us would be proud to sign our name to. And has it paid off for Linux? You bet.

The Linux-based Apache Web server software is used to run 60 percent of the world's Web sites.[6] Software company V. A. Linux saw its stock soar from $30 to $239 the first day it was offered, the largest first-day gain of any IPO in stock market history. Linux-based Redhat offered small allocations of its difficult-to-obtain IPO stock to passionate, influential volunteer programmers as a thank you. The stock tripled in value on its first day and continued to climb thereafter.[7]

How Passionate are Your Most Admired?

Go back to your most admired list of individuals (page 19). On the scale below, circle the number that represents your best guess at the level of each person's passion for his or her work. Use one circle for each person.

Look at the individuals in the 7 to 10 range on the scale. What makes them passionate about their work? If you don't know and have access to them, ask them why they get excited about their work.

- Is it the field in which they work?
- Is it the type of job?
- Is it the people they work with?

Although each person's work may be different, it is likely that the reasons for being passionate are similar. Based on the people you selected and their characteristics, what are three insights you have about your own passion at work?

1. _____

2. _____

3. _____

So what about you? Are you like Linux programmers who find it hard to distinguish between work and play? Or, when you get home at nighht, are you thinking, "Thank God that's over. I can get on with living"? If you feel trapped and flee work instead of leaving it to go home, are you aware that you can have the same sort of love affair with your work as

Alberto Giacometti had? It is possible because, although someone else may control your pay stub, ultimately you work for you. You're the boss of the passion you have for your work . . . and your job is to uncover it.

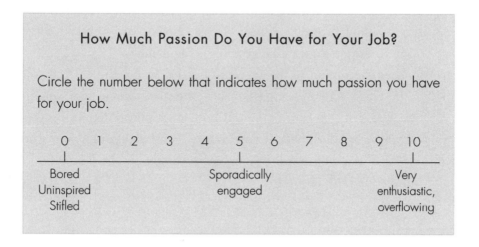

Love the Job You're With

HOW YOU WORK and, more important, how you feel about work—as people like Judy George, Howard Schultz, and Tony LePore prove—is very much in your hands. Like our dancing traffic cop, maybe you grew up wanting to be a performer, but a host of real-life variables "got in the way."

Why not, like LePore, choose to find your rhythm within the chaos of horns and cars in your life, a rhythm to which you can choreograph your unique and personal dance? A rhythm that might land you spots on *The Rosie O'Donnell Show* and *Dateline*, or in a movie or radio commercials as it did our man in blue. A rhythm that might lead to an autobiography and might have the mayor of Providence pull you out of retirement once a year during the holidays to cheer up the city because you are missed so very much. A rhythm that might just possibly get you where you wanted to go in the first place.

When you think of it, most of us stumbled into the jobs we have. It's a rare teenager or even young adult who knows exactly what he or she wants to become as a grown-up and then becomes it. Of those who did, many regret their choices. For example, many of us have known students who from the beginning aspired to be doctors. Yet, research reveals that 40 percent of physicians are dissatisfied with medicine as a career.[8] So if you're berating yourself because of past choices you've made, forget it. You have the option to change things. Right now.

You have the option to do the work needed to tap the core of your being, the place where your passion lies, the place where the "you" in *you* lies. The first step is to figure out how to amplify whatever residual passion you've got and make it grow into a flame that guides your work in the future. Each of us has passion somewhere. The trick is to find it and build your work around it.

Managing Passion

TO ME PASSION is motivation with a soul. How many times have I heard an exasperated manager bemoan the fact that a particular employee was "not motivated"?

When I was just starting out in the training business, Ann, one of the professionals in our company, was counseling Allan, a frustrated supervisor. Allan stated that trying to motivate a particular employee, Ray, was like trying to make moss on a tree grow faster. Ann listened to his tale of woe with her characteristic empathy and then asked three questions:

Q: Is there anything at all that appears to motivate Ray outside of work?

A: Yes, he always talks about his volunteer work with young children at the YMCA. I gather he is quite good at it. Even won an award.

Q: What makes Ray so successful at the YMCA?

A: Well, he tells me he created the program for the kids and was able to take a risk or two in getting it off the ground.

Q: Coaching, creativity, and risk taking seem to be the keys to motivating Ray at the Y. Do you encourage him to do the same at work?

Bingo! Allan got it immediately. As a micromanager he had stifled Ray's natural enthusiasm for the task by telling him exactly what to do and controlling his actions, rather than inviting him to bring his own creativity into play. In fact, it was Allan's oversupervising that was causing the problem, not Ray's lack of motivation.

Tapping the passion in others can be a powerful management tool. Everyone is motivated by something. Maybe it's not by the current conditions at work—the money, the manager, the recognition, the task, or the career track—but everyone is either intrinsically or extrinsically motivated by something. Intrinsic motivation comes in the form of such internal rewards as a sense of accomplishment, enhanced confidence, and the chance to grow. Extrinsic motivations are those external rewards that provide tangible or publicly recognized enticements such as money, position, and power. Discerning the particular extrinsic or intrinsic sources of motivation can ultimately lead to work most suitable to bringing out the best each of us has to offer. But more important, they may provide clues to where the heart of unrealized passion resides.

How to Capture Passion

THINK OF A time in your life when you were totally engaged and happy. It could be at work, at home, or in any other circumstance. This was probably a moment when you totally lost track of time.

1. What were you doing and feeling at that time? Identify those precise activities and situations that give you the most excitement and enthusiasm.

2. How can you change the nature and content of your work to incorporate more of what you identified in the above? Invent ways to do your job so that it will include more of the activities that naturally engage you.

If Ray—the employee who was doing great things with the children at the YMCA but was finding less enjoyment at work—was doing this exercise he might consider the following actions to incorporate creativity, pioneering, and coaching into his work:

1. Ask his manager if he could be allowed time to mentor some of the newer employees.
2. Ask his manager for the latitude to stretch past business-as-usual and test creative ways to improve whatever work processes comprise his job.

Making Motivation into Passion

The questions Ann asked of the frustrated supervisor were not complex, but it's the simple questions that often provide the most profound answers. Respond to the questions below and place your answers in either the *Extrinsic* or *Intrinsic* column as appropriate.

1. What motivates you at work, if anything? What gives you pleasure? What feels as if it's just necessary?
2. What motivates you outside of work, if anything? Gives you pleasure? Feels necessary?

Extrinsic Motivators	Intrinsic Motivators

3. As you consider these questions and record your answers, take notice of the subtle but powerful forces that drive you, that give you great satisfaction and pleasure, that make you lose track of time. Equally important, note those that have the opposite effect. By defining what doesn't work for you, you'll be better equipped to articulate what does.

4. Review your list of extrinsic and intrinsic motivators. Which ones hold the most power for you? Those will be the ones that are the gateway to your passion.

Passion Is a Balancing Act

BELOW IS FRAMEWORK for assessing your job and determining what elements you need to change in order to move toward the perfect occupation. Each work situation is composed of four components:

1. What I do well. This represents those skills and areas of mastery that you have demonstrated in past circumstances. These could include such competencies as interpersonal skills, artistic flair, proficiency with numbers, planning ability, writing talent, athletic prowess, and the like.

2. What I can get paid. Either people will pay you for doing something or they won't. Or they'll pay, but not at a level to sustain the lifestyle you want. Many musicians, artisans, and athletes, for example, are extraordinarily talented, but opportunities to play out their passions full-time are scarce, and the competition for those opportunities is frenetic. Often such artists are forced to augment subsistence pay with "real" jobs.

3. What I can learn. When you are learning you are growing, and when you are growing you are more likely to be excited, fulfilled, and energized. Conversely, imagine how dreadful it would be to work at a job that offers zero opportunity to grow in knowledge or skills. It is the difference between regenerative versus degenerative work, that is, the difference between work that gives back and work that only takes.

4. What I love doing. This is where the passion comes in. I have a friend, a lawyer, who is an expert on medieval canon law. When she talks about her avocation, her entire demeanor changes. Her eyes twinkle, she talks more excitedly and she is much more animated. She would like this to be her vocation, but, in spite of her strong passion and deep knowledge of this esoteric subject, no one will pay her enough to pursue it.

The Four-Ring Analysis

THE KEY TO success in work is to have all four of the above elements in balance. As you can see from the illustration below, the extent to which these four factors overlap indicates the extent to which you have found the best job for you. They will overlap when they are in relative balance. For example, John recently told me he is very happy at work. When I asked why, he responded: "First off, I love what I'm doing [passion] and I'm really having an impact [well]. The money's good [$], and I'm being challenged to do new things all the time [learn]."

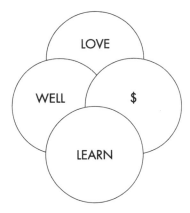

In the ideal situation they will overlap to the point that they appear to be only one circle:

Of course, what happens to most of us is that these four circles do not overlap so much as cascade into a hierarchy of perceived importance. The primary component is usually *money*, followed by *skills*, followed by *learning*, and finally, *passion*. This hierarchy is a trap.

Without Passion, Having It All Isn't Enough

THE RESIDENT INVESTMENT guru for a prestigious global financial services firm who is a frequently featured guest on the financial news channel CNBC, couldn't agree more. He is a highly esteemed "rainmaker" and great at what he does. He loves the money he makes, the car he drives, the vacations he takes, the wine he puts in the cellar . . . but deep down he can't stand his work. If he trusted you, he would confide that, yes, he feels absolutely trapped by the material things upon which he has become dependent. He is put off by the politics, the pettiness, the grasping of the people he works with. He dislikes his company; what it values; how it operates. The fact is that his golden handcuffs may look pretty, but they are handcuffs just the same. His circles are way out of whack.

Align Your Circles

THE GREATER THE balance of money, skills, learning, and passion, the better the work situation. There is a way to determine what you need to do to achieve greater balance.

1. Using a scale of 0 to 10, list the satisfaction level for each of your four circles, "0" being miserable, "5" being satisfied, and "10" being ecstatic. Total the four numbers. If you scored a 40, your circles are in complete alignment. You have found the perfect job for you. If you don't have a 40, identify the circle with the biggest gap and start there. Identify what is missing or what needs to be eliminated to get to a 10. Be as specific as possible.
2. Brainstorm actions you can take to resolve the sources of dissatisfaction. Here are some ideas to get you started:

What I Do Well
- Look for opportunities to apply your unique talents by volunteering for assignments that will allow you to utilize them.
- If possible, minimize the menial aspects of your work through technology or enlisting the support of others.

What I Get Paid
- Identify higher-paying jobs you can strive for and determine with your manager what you need to do to qualify for them.
- Focus on those performance targets whose achievement will create the greatest opportunity for a salary increase or bonus.

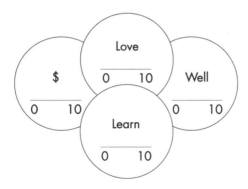

What I Learn

- Seek new opportunities for collateral assignments that will allow you to stretch.
- Find a coach or mentor to help you with the parts of your work with which you are least familiar.

What I Love

- Reflect on the previous exercise on pages 27–28, and invent ways to bring more of what you love doing into your current job.
- Find the good in the bad by discovering how you can experience more enjoyment while doing the requisite mundane parts of your job. Think of adding background music or turning it into a game such as beating the clock.

With Passion, Less Can Be More

IT HAS BEEN said, "Money isn't everything, but it sure greases the wheels." Money can, in fact, buy happiness if it is used for the purposes of passion. For example, forty-seven-year-old Steve Hoffman made a ton of money during his twenty-one-year career at Sugarman & Sugarman, a prestigious Boston law firm. He made enough money to start working for what would be peanuts by his former standards. He quit his job at Sugarman and signed on as a lowly assistant district attorney for the

princely sum of $28,000 a year. Now, despite a shabby office and gruel-
ing hours, he's doing what he absolutely loves and cares most about—
public service. Says Hoffman: "You have a nice home, live in a safe
community, and have enough money to put the kids through college,
that's it. What else do you need? What's important to me is that my
kids see their parents do meaningful work."[9] Money and success paved
a path for Hoffman to follow his passion.

I'm not denigrating money, success, and power. But if your passion
lies elsewhere, these achievements will seem meaningless. Richard Edler, author of *If I Knew Then What I Know Now*, spent six years gathering
hindsights from numerous CEOs and other professional leaders. They
each answered the same single question: "What do you know now that
you wish someone had told you twenty-five years ago?" The most frequent response was "I wish I had followed my dream." Established business leaders, all of them wealthy high achievers, were looking back on
their lives and lamenting the fact that although they had done extremely
well, something was missing. And that something was passion.

Another survey of "successful" veteran businesspeople indicates the
same thing, but with a twist. It wasn't just sheer passion that was missing.
It was passion rooted by purpose.

Richard Leider, author, executive coach, and founder of the Inven-
ture Group, interviewed more than 1,000 retirees who had carved out
distinguished careers. Says Leider: "I think it was Oliver Wendell
Holmes who said, 'Most of us go to our graves with our music still inside
us.' Many of these people felt that, despite their successes, their music
was still inside them. . . . If they could live their lives over again, they
would understand what really gave them fulfillment. You might call this
the power of purpose: doing something that contributes to life, adding
value to life beyond yourself."[10]

Passion is important. It creates energy, but purpose focuses and shapes
it. Purpose can have greater power when it is outside yourself, beyond
your ego or your financial self-interest.

DISCOVER YOUR PURPOSE

We can't run away from who we are. Our destiny chooses us.

— Martin Landau,
Rounders

PRESUMABLY, MOST PARENTS raise their children to do well in school, and regard report cards as one measure of how well they are parenting. Modern guru Deepak Chopra sees it differently. He wasn't big on academic ratings as an indication of success for his children. When his children were in their formative years, Chopra saw his job as helping them discover what they were passionate about. He did this by giving them the freedom and space to try and perhaps fail before they happened upon it. Once they found their passion, he then advised them to find a way to use that passion *in service to others*. Clearly the wisdom behind this loving counsel was that passion needs a reason that goes beyond Self. It needs a purpose.

Yet most people don't know their life purpose. In fact, many have really never thought about it. When they are asked to identify their purpose they often get caught up in their "lack" of purpose and think of themselves as being incomplete or unenlightened. Their response is often a sheepish, "No I don't have one. I guess I should, don't you think?"

If they don't worry about their "lack" of purpose, they may discount their life purpose if it doesn't feel as substantial as Mother Teresa's or Gandhi's. The key to finding your life purpose is remembering that it is personal to you. Executive secretary Pam Oesterlin says that hers is to "be a great mom"; business executive Charles Eitel says he wants "to help people discover their courage and be the best they can be";[11] successful author and speaker Marcia Wieder says her purpose is "to joyously express." Comparisons are irrelevant.

Life has been described as a tapestry that we only see from the back. On rare occasions, the tapestry is turned around and we see how all the threads are woven together. So if you have no idea what your life purpose is, relax. That's perfectly okay and common. If you never consciously discover your so-called reason for being, it doesn't mean you don't have one and won't find passion at work. And if you come closer to discovering your purpose, it will help inspire your passion.

One way to think of your life purpose is to think of it as a kind of personal vision. In the past few years, corporate visioning has become one of the top tools used by business leaders to create a cohesive and determined work group, and to focus and inspire people to accomplish more. A vision is powerful because it usually embraces those elements that people care about most—meaningful work, personal growth, and a tangible, soul-satisfying goal.

It is said that people at work are motivated, in reverse order of importance, by the following three factors: money, great leadership, and having a cause. People are certainly motivated by a paycheck, but great leadership will have an even more rousing effect. Having a cause beats both the paycheck and the leader hands down. People will make extraordinary commitments and sacrifices for what they consider a true cause. At work you have your pay, and your leader-manager, but do you have a cause? This is the vision of your organization and can represent a powerful motivating force for you and your workmates.

Proof of the power of vision is offered by research conducted by Stanford Business School professors Jerry Porras and James Collins. As reported in *Built to Last*, Porras and Collins tracked the stock performance of both average and visionary companies and compared their economic performance. Since 1926, the stock value of visionary companies—that is, companies that operated with a clear set of visions and values, whether expressed or implied—outperformed their nonvisionary counterparts, on average, by a ratio of fifteen to one.

If a vision can have such a positive, long-term influence on a company, just imagine what it can do for your life.

Create a Vision for Your Work

MANY OF US have been involved in writing vision statements for our company, our department, or an organization we volunteer for on a regular basis. This exercise will help you create a vision for your work and a springboard for discovering your life purpose in a later exercise.

1. Think of yourself as a supplier to customers. Consider the work products and services you routinely deliver to them. Your customers are people either inside or outside your company to whom you pass your work.
   Answer the following questions:

   • What do I deliver to my customers?
   • How does what I deliver to my customers create value for them?
   • How does what I deliver to my customers create value for *their* customers?
   • What would happen if I started to deliver low-quality work products and services to my customers?

2. A good vision is not simply an objective description of *what you actually do*, but rather of what *you deliver* that is important to others and helps them do a better job. Considering the answers to the questions above, and any other thoughts you may have about your work, write a vision statement for your job. Try to limit your statement to no more than twenty-five words.

3. See if you can distill your twenty-five-word vision into a few words or a short phrase. The most powerful vision statements are brief. Big corporations understand the impact of brevity and have vision statements like "Quality is Job 1" (Ford); "To create a place where we can all be kids" (Disney Theme Parks); "We are ladies and gentlemen serving ladies and gentlemen" (Ritz Carlton Hotels). Go ahead and try it. You may want to start with the words "My vision for my job is . . ."

Testing Your Vision

HOW WILL YOUR vision statement perform for you? Answer the following questions:

1. Do you feel excited when you think about your job in terms of your vision statement?
2. Do you feel good about the value of your work?
3. Does your vision statement open up new ideas about performing your job?
4. Does your vision support the vision of your work unit and organization?

If you answered "No" to any of these questions, rewrite your vision so that you can answer "Yes."

From Vision to Purpose

NOW THAT YOU have created a vision for your work, it's time to start thinking about your life purpose. A vision statement is a verbal picture of what you wish to achieve in the relatively short term. In this case, you have created a vision for your job. From time to time you might revise this picture based on changing conditions and circumstances. Your life purpose, on the other hand, is more permanent and far-reaching than your vision. It is intrinsic to your core and is your raison d'être, your reason to be.

Discover Your Purpose

THE FOLLOWING EXERCISE can help you discover your life purpose:

1. Answer the following question: To what do I dedicate my life? The answer needn't be eloquent or lofty, just personally important. Remem-

ber Pam's "to be a great mom," or Charlie's "to help people discover their courage and be the best they can be"? What is important is that the response be truly yours and not influenced by the expectations others may have or have had for you. Another way of thinking about this question is to ask yourself: If I could be remembered for one contribution in my life, what would it be?

2. Based on your answer, compose a one-sentence description of your life purpose. Use words that have power and meaning for you. State this sentence in terms of what you are here to do — what you will accomplish rather than what you will avoid. For example, "I will have a positive impact on the lives of my friends and family," rather than, "I will avoid hurting my friends and family." Even if the words do not come easily, try to write something down. You can always change it later.

After completing a similar exercise to the one above, I was able to discover my life purpose: "to help bring spirit back to business." Once I had that clarified, I was able to start living life on purpose. That insight profoundly changed everything about my life because suddenly I had a touchstone from which to quickly gauge those activities that moved me toward my purpose and, equally important, those that didn't. I focused my speaking and workshops on new topics, read different work-related books, established new relationships, attended different conferences, volunteered for different assignments and even interacted with my workmates differently.

Knowing your life purpose gives you the ability to manage your life with pristine clarity and confident decisiveness. Once that happens the only question is whether or not you will have the courage to pursue what is consistent with it, and get rid of what isn't.

Refining Your Purpose

NOW THAT YOU have a first draft of your life purpose, let's look at a way to refine it. Our friends and relatives often see us more clearly than we see ourselves. This exercise involves getting their insight. Although you may not be aware of your life purpose, you may still be living it, and sometimes commentary from independent observers can help you realize that which you cannot see.

1. Select several friends and/or relatives who know you well and whom you believe will give you respectful and candid information about yourself. Interview at least three or up to five such people.

2. Start with the person you trust the most. Tell him or her what you are trying to accomplish with the interview and ask the questions listed below. Repeat the process with the others. In order to remember what is said, you may want to take notes or tape-record the responses.

Your job is to gather the honest thoughts from these friends or relatives. Avoid defending or arguing. Rather, just quietly take in the information as they speak. Only ask additional questions when you want something explained or expanded:

1. "I am thinking about how I can bring my work and my life purpose closer together. But because I am too close to some of the issues surrounding it, I thought your objective observations could be helpful to me."
2. "Based on what I do, how I spend my time, and what I appear to value, what are some of the things that seem to be important to me in my life?"
3. "When do I seem happiest? What do you think it is that makes me so happy?"
4. "What do you see me avoiding or not enjoying?"
5. "Imagine I were no longer on this earth and someone asked you what I stood for, what would it be?"
6. "Understanding that you're not an expert on life purpose, if you were guessing at mine, what do you think it would be?"

Based on these interviews, rewrite your life purpose as appropriate. You have now created and refined your life purpose. List how your current job supports the achievement of that purpose. Also note how it might be in conflict. What can you do to better align your job and purpose?

Awareness of your passion and purpose will help you start realizing the best there is for your life and your job. Perhaps this knowledge may ultimately lead you to chart an entirely new career path. But what about the here and now? Pragmatically, what can you do immediately to start reaping the benefits of your discoveries about your passion and also, perhaps, your purpose?

You can start by reengineering your job.

REENGINEER YOUR JOB

Passionate choices have potent consequences.

—JANA KOLPEN,
The Secrets of Pistoulet

IN 1992, I was president of a division in our company and found myself in a situation where my "four circles" had fallen out of alignment. My income was reasonable; I was doing my work with considerable proficiency; I was still learning in some areas; but the passion was dwindling. As it did, the misalignment became increasingly painful. Tasks that I had previously reveled in, like managing people, had become monotonous and burdensome.

Realizing this, I made a "plus and minus" assessment, a process often attributed to Ben Franklin. This involves taking a fresh sheet of paper and drawing a vertical line down the middle. On the left side I wrote "PLUS" and recorded everything I loved about my work. This included public speaking, writing, mentoring, and marketing. On the right I wrote "MINUS" and included everything I didn't love, such as budgeting, managing, office politics, and attending meetings. When I was done, there were five items on my PLUS list and eight in the MINUS column. I then deliberately set out to create a way to have more of the pluses and less of the minuses to bring my work situation into balance.

This process didn't come without stress, however. For example, I gave up my job as division president and all the prestige and perks that went with it. I cut my work time at the company to half, with a commensurate 50 percent reduction in income (that was, I admit, a little frightening). As a result of these actions my influence in company operations was lessened. But in this trade-off I retained those things I most enjoyed, while freeing up half my time to pursue new directions. These actions were voluntary on my part and, although laced with uncertainty and even some fear, they were refreshingly invigorating. I reengineered my work and the passion was back! The following approach will help you determine what you can do to reengineer your job.

Reengineer Time and Task

THERE ARE FIVE steps you can take to modify what you do. You can:

1. Do *more* of something.
2. Do *less* of something.
3. *Stop* doing something.
4. *Start* doing something.
5. Do something *differently*.

Do More

DAN, THE TECHNOLOGY manager of a high-tech corporation, recognized that one powerful marketing activity in his industry was being virtually ignored by his company. Dan noticed that at trade association meetings, marketing events, and other venues, his competitors would send in "experts" to speak on various topics of interest to audiences of prospective customers. Although competitors were using this tactic to great effect, no one was adept at public speaking at Dan's company.

Dan's enthusiasm for the idea far outweighed his speaking prowess. While he was good with small groups, the idea of addressing a larger group of potential customers was daunting. Still, driven by the vision of increased sales through new relationships, he decided to take the job on. He put the word out to his sales force that he would be willing to travel anywhere in the country to make a presentation to existing customers. If they could muster more than twenty people, he would show up and do his thing free of charge. The only caveat was that the topic would have to lie within his area of expertise.

After several weeks Dan had his first taker. A salesperson "sold" him into a 30-person presentation. Dan immediately sprang into action. He refined his knowledge of the topic through research, designed his presentation, and created the supporting audiovisuals. At the same time he read two books on public speaking and, after practicing his presentation five times, did a dry run in front of a small group of staff members from his office. He videotaped this session and then critiqued his own performance with several others in order to fine-tune it.

The result of all this preparation was a powerful presentation from which customers received great value. The word got out to the rest of the sales force and soon Dan's phone was ringing off the hook. He went on to become a powerful spokesperson for his company at industry meetings and positively affected its sales. An activity that was formerly limited to occasional internal presentations expanded to occupy almost 40 percent of his time. Dan found new passion for his work by being ready and making himself able to take on additional challenges.

Do Less

MY GUESS IS that paperwork, whether actual or electronic, is something most of us would readily consign to the "less" category. Nowhere is this more likely to be true than in a sales organization. Historically, salespeople have considered administrative tasks to be an intrusion on their real selling time—the time spent with customers. This could not have been more true for Henry, a business equipment salesperson. Henry loved selling but hated the paperwork that went with it. So he set out to find ways to eliminate or reduce it. The questions he asked were, "What are my administrative tasks?" "In which do I spend the most time?" and "How can I reduce time spent in these tasks?"

Since he was responsible for creating his own sales leads he was required to do a lot of telephone prospecting. This required identifying potential customers, securing contact information, sending an introductory letter, and then calling for an appointment. After scheduling an appointment he would then send a confirmation letter. After he actually made the sales call, depending on what had transpired, he would write follow-up letters. By the time he was done, Henry had sunk a large amount of precious "customer face time" in his office researching and composing customized letters.

Henry decided to act. He trained his administrative assistant to do the prospecting. Incidentally, in the process of doing this, he enriched his assistant's job. She took great pride in culling the opportunities and coming up with a high-quality "hit list."

After analyzing his correspondence, Henry realized that there were seven different types of letters that covered 85 percent of his letter-writing situations. He created two stock letters that could be customized by cutting-and-pasting a variety of precomposed paragraphs as appropriate. After his assistant adapted the stock letters as needed, all Henry had to do was add a personal note and signature. Not only did Henry end up spending more time doing what he really loved—seeing customers— and less time on paperwork, reengineering his job to do less also had the great benefit of increasing sales.

Stop Doing Something

JANE, EXECUTIVE VICE president of a large services firm, typically spent a solid hour and a half in her car commuting to and from work. Jane reasoned that by working out of her home on days that did not require her presence in the office, not only did she avoid a numbing and time-wasting commute but she also became more productive and less stressed.

Nick, a salesperson on the West Coast, was not making the numbers he believed he should. He analyzed the situation and discovered that he spent the same amount of time closing an account whether it was large or small. The large account was a better deal, however, because the initial order was bigger and there was the opportunity for many reorders with less incremental selling time. His decision? Hardly brilliant, but most telling. Focus exclusively on the larger ones. With this "personal work stoppage" he became the most productive salesperson in his office.

Start Doing Something

SUSAN HAD BEEN an administrative assistant for over a year when she started discussing additional areas of work with her manager. She was primarily interested in marketing, so it was arranged for her to be involved in an occasional marketing project. Although this arrangement allowed her to try her hand at something new and interesting, her work with her manager was established as the top priority. This situation ended up being a win for everyone. The marketing department was delighted to have an occasional extra pair of hands, Susan was excited to be learning marketing, and her manager continued to have a happy and productive assistant. In fact, things worked out so well that a year later when a new opening came up in the marketing department, they made a beeline for Susan.

If you have gotten clear on the things you like doing and those that you don't, then having a discussion with your manager about adding new responsibilities can be productive and even life-changing.

Some managers are very willing to have a reengineering discussion, while others feel threatened. If yours is the latter, think of ways to present your proposal so that your manager will clearly perceive how your taking on additional work will both benefit the manager and the company.

Getting Your Boss on Your Side

WHEN YOU START tinkering with the various components of your job it is generally a good idea to do it with the support of your manager. Your performance contract, after all is with him or her and your company. It seems fair to agree on any changes that could jeopardize expected outcomes. Plus, you will enhance the chances of successfully reengineering your job if you have your boss supporting you. Below are some hints to help make this happen:

- In all your discussions, demonstrate how your proposed changes will increase the likelihood of meeting performance targets.
- While you're at it, find ways to demonstrate how your job changes will eliminate headaches for, and ensure the success of, your manager.
- Look for other examples where your manager has adapted the work situation of others. Ask yourself, What were the conditions that allowed that to happen? How can I create similar conditions?
- Always present your ideas in terms of benefits. How will it pay off for all involved?
- Rather than requesting a permanent change, propose that you "try it out" for a quarter or two and see how it works. That way you are not asking your manager to make an irrevocable commitment.
- Check with your human resources department (if you have one) to discover similar precedents you can use to strengthen your case.

- Identify those aspects of your job you can change without your manager's consent and change them.
- If all fails and you don't have a supportive manager, consider the risks in making the changes anyway. This will be an all or nothing gamble. If it works you may look like a hero. If it doesn't, well, it may mean a black mark in your personnel folder.

Do Something Differently

FRED WAS ONE of the leading salespeople in his company. He had been with the firm for several years and had established himself as a reliable performer. His wife, Jennifer, also had a demanding job that she performed with equal proficiency.

Their job demands were such that their children were starting to lose out. Fred and Jennifer decided that one of them was going to have to change his or her work situation. Fred did. He approached his manager and was granted the option of working a four-day week. The only condition was that his production not fall behind. Says Fred, "The funny thing was, although I was working less, I was more effective, motivated, and focused. I ended up having my best year ever." Fred asked for and received permission to do his job differently, but, as he points out, he had "earned the right" by performing well previously. The better you perform, the more valuable you are to your company, and the more likely accommodations will be made for you.

Chances are the reengineering of time and task will help you bring more fresh air into your work situation. No matter what the results of that effort, however, reengineering your attitude toward your job may end up paying the biggest dividends of all.

The Start, Stop, More, Less, Differently decision-making framework will be presented at the end of each chapter in this book under the heading "Action Steps." The purpose is to help you convert the insight you gained by reading the chapter into specific, job-enhancing actions.

If a journey of a thousand miles starts with a single step, then this framework can help you figure out what first steps to take.

In this chapter we have presented three actions you can take to follow your passion. They are:

1. Uncover your passion.
2. Discover your purpose.
3. Reengineer your job.

All three are mutually supporting. Passion creates energy; purpose directs it; and reengineering enables you to focus on those parts of your job that have the highest personal payoff while reducing or eliminating those that do not. Together these three actions will be of immeasurable help as you follow your passion.

Start/Stop/More/Less/Different

1. In the two columns below record all aspects of your job that give you satisfaction (PLUS) and those that are negative (MINUS).

+ PLUS	– MINUS

2. Looking at each item in your PLUS and MINUS columns, what can you Start, Stop, Do More, Do Less, or Do Differently in order to eliminate or minimize the negative aspects of your job and increase the satisfaction you derive from it? Use your imagination, and don't

reject any action out of hand until you are absolutely certain it won't work.

- I will start . . .

  _____

  _____

  _____

- I will stop . . .

  _____

  _____

  _____

- I will do more . . .

  _____

  _____

  _____

- I will do less . . .

  _____

  _____

  _____

- I will do differently . . .

  _____

  _____

  _____

Be Home

*All of life is a coming home. Salesmen. Secretaries. Coal
miners. Beekeepers. Sword swallowers. All of us . . . all the
restless hearts of the world . . . all trying to find a way
home.*

— PATCH ADAMS

IT HAD BEEN one of those "it doesn't get any better than this"
kinds of days. Skiing with my sons. Jackson Hole. Blue sky. Fresh pow-
der. Short lines. And then, in a split second, everything turned ugly.
Suddenly I was teetering on a desolate precipice there in Wyoming,
perched precariously between a rock and a cliff—fear and panic, life
and death.

I was so far from home . . . and yet it was there that I realized the life-
altering and, perhaps, life-saving power of being able to instantaneously
return—from whatever or wherever—to that most familiar, safe, and
grounded place called home.

Of course, when we think of "home," it's usually a physical location
that comes to mind—most likely the house you live in or perhaps the
one you loved as a child. The home I refer to, however, is different. It's
the home within all of us. It's that place where inner peace and incredible strength and clarity reside. Call it what you will—inner harmony,

your center, the soul. No matter. The fact is that all cultures and beliefs affirm its intangible but certain reality.

Just where is this very special home and how do you access it? Opinions vary. Saint Augustine thought it was in the blood. René Descartes believed it was in "a certain very small gland in the middle of the brain."[1] Practitioners of chi kung call it the *dan tiem* and place it one or two inches below the navel; yoga teachers refer to it as your *hara*; and transcendental meditators find it by shifting into an alpha state.

Perhaps no one puts it better than Rabbi Zalman Schachter-Shalomi, who describes it this way: "My daughter once asked me, 'Abba, when you're asleep, you can wake up, right?' I said yes. She said, 'When you're awake, can you wake up even more?' Soul is where we awaken even more."[2]

In times of stress, in order to find this place, many of us have learned how to "count to ten" or "chill." When we see people in this state we use terms like "flow" or "in the zone." Whatever the descriptive phrase, there does seem to be this home within each of us that can be a potent source of power and calmness, of resilience and adaptability, of crystal-clear judgment and the wonderful ability to feel and act naturally. When we access this place, we have the intriguing possibility of going to work and being home at the same time. Or going to a social event and being home. Or even more interesting, going home and being home.

In times when we are free from stress, this ability to be home can occur unbidden — and instantly transform us into a peak performer. When this happens we often use phrases like "in the groove," "on autopilot," "cooking," and "hyperfocused." Think of a basketball player pouring in three-pointers from incredible distances — unconscious, in the zone, just doing naturally what his innate ability, freed of fear and doubt, will allow him to do. When we perform in such an elevated state, it has little to do with the mind. We just seem to arrive there when conditions are right. And when we arrive, no matter what we are doing, the pure performer shows up — confident, clear, decisive, and ready to act.

I am reminded of a special events coordinator from a major high-tech firm I saw in action recently. She and her staff were responsible for the flawless coordination and running of a three-day global partner meeting. Her "to-do" list consisted of such activities as supervising the meeting producers, coaching the company's executives, "hand-holding" the guest speakers, registering the 4,000 certified resellers, coordinating meals and other logistics, changing individual travel arrangements, and cheerfully responding to every unanticipated problem with swiftness and effectiveness. If ever there was grace under fire this was it. With incredible coolness she stayed centered at the middle of the chaos, calmly issuing directives, adapting, correcting, finding alternative solutions, even smiling and joking with the practiced ease of a mom getting her children off to school.

This maestra of mayhem was 1,200 miles from her house but, clearly, she was also home. Like the sharpshooting basketball player, she was fully engaged with all her resources focused on the task at hand. She was experiencing that high that I call home, of being in the zone of preparedness and adaptability, utter focus on split-second happenings, and unruffled bobbing and weaving through unexpected obstacles. We've all felt it, and when we do, whether alone or with others, we know that the world is getting the absolute best we have to offer.

What Does "Home" Feel Like?

- Think of a time when you had a crisis at work and handled it with coolness, assurance, and great effectiveness. How did you feel? What did you do or think to remain calm?

- Now think of a time when you had a crisis at work and panicked, lost it. How did you feel? What could you have done to react more effectively?

The difference between the two situations is the difference between being home . . . and being lost. What can you learn from this brief analysis of your ability to be home?

Can one *intentionally* access this magical place, the home that dwells within? Yes, although in truth there is no surefire formula. What we can do, however, is create the circumstances in which this is more likely to occur. In so doing, we'll improve our ability to perform whether we achieve being home completely or not. There are a number of ways to access this place. Three that many find help immeasurably are:

1. Find your center.
2. Be present.
3. Detach from outcomes.

These three are not the only ways to find your way back home. They are simply the ones that I rely upon and hope you will find just as useful, in order to experience a more confident, joyous, and productive work life.

FIND YOUR CENTER

MOMENTUM WAS THE problem at Jackson Hole. I had veered off onto a remote narrow path that fed me straight to the mountain's edge. A small gully trapped my skis in such a way that the only way to free them was to rock back and forth. Too little momentum and I'd go nowhere. Too much and *sayonara*. I'd fly over a three-story cliff to the jagged rocks below, which seemed as menacing as the gaping maw of a great white shark. My physical well-being was a matter of inches, and every decision, every move, was critical.

I closed my eyes, breathed deeply, relaxed my shoulders and found my center of gravity—that spot just below my navel. As I did this, my throat relaxed, my legs stopped shaking and my feet and skis once again felt comfortably rooted. Most important, the fear subsided. My predicament hadn't gone away, but now I could begin to think clearly and act decisively. I was home.

The lens of fear had been focusing my attention only on the threatening rocks below and to images of my demise: of my spread-eagled lifeless body splayed across them. Now, however, with my composure restored, I was able to stop obsessing about the problem and start looking for a solution.

And there it was, a way out — a barely visible narrow path, lightly etched into the face of the precipice. Although it appeared no wider than the width of a bicycle tire, as I lifted each ski over the modest bump in front of me — with cautious but steady movements — the trail began to open up. I felt like an airplane descending from white-knuckle turbulence into the arms of an ever-widening runway.

As I slid safely onto the awaiting slope with its beautiful, white, fluffy, soft snow, it struck me how concrete, practical, and potentially life-altering the capacity to be home is. My ability to center, to be home at that perilous moment, certainly saved me from serious injury and may have even saved my life. I learned that being home is not simply a feel-good, ethereal concept. It is real power.

How to Center

MOST OF US don't want to wait until a desperate moment like staring down a cliff before we learn to center ourselves. The following three basics will get you centering right now with breath control, balance, and the ability to root.

1. Diaphragmatic breathing. Breathing is where it all begins. Stop for a moment and take three belly breaths right now. Sit with your back straight, shoulders relaxed, and feet flat on the floor. Then, as *slowly and deeply* as possible, inhale through your nose and exhale through your mouth. These are called "belly breaths," because when done properly the lower reaches of the lungs are so fully extended that the air pressure pushes out the lower stomach. When was the last time you breathed like that? As you do, feel the tension leave and the energy arrive.

Expand your lung capacity by progressively extending the time it takes to inhale and exhale. Record your times for each in/out phase as well as for each full cycle and keep trying to beat your own record.

2. *Balance*. Stand with your feet apart at shoulder width, knees slightly bent. Shift your weight slightly back and forth until you find that place where you feel complete equilibrium. Do the same thing again but this time rock gently from side to side instead. Use these subtle counter-motions to keep your balance in check.

Often what feels like balance to us isn't quite what it seems to be, and we are off center a bit. Ask someone to examine your stance from the front, back, and each side and note where you may unknowingly be out of alignment. Make the adjustments recommended by your partner and remain in this aligned position for a minute or two. With practice, you will learn to find this balanced position instantly and at will.

3. *Root*. Stand with your feet at shoulder width and knees slightly flexed. Locate a spot about 1½ inches below your navel and touch it gently with your fingers. This is your physical and energetic center. Now imagine you are a giant oak tree with strong entrenched roots extending from the bottoms of your feet deep down into the earth. Practice doing this several times a day until this rooted position feels natural and familiar and you are able to return to it with nothing more than a passing "oak tree" thought.

Have a friend *very* gently and gradually push against your upper chest with one hand until you lose your balance. Now try it again, but instead of resisting by leaning forward, allow your body to adapt itself to the unyielding oak tree image as described above. Did either of you notice any difference?

When you face a challenging situation at work, find your center by using this breathe, balance, and root technique.

Centering at Work

*Nothing gives one person so great advantage over another
as to remain always cool and unruffled under all circumstances.*

— THOMAS JEFFERSON[3]

HE'S GRUFF, MYOPIC, inflexible, impatient, quick to judge, hard to
please, bears a striking resemblance to *It's a Wonderful Life*'s Old Man
Potter—and he's *your* boss. And yes, it's annual performance review
time.

Mr. Potter, as is his way, has not taken the time to observe you in
action or gather all of the necessary data from others who are more
conversant with the reality of your day-to-day performance. You are also
sure he has taken a couple of incidents involving you out of context
and, as a result, has formed a negative view of what you have achieved.

The morning of the big event, you dress smartly and adopt your most
professional demeanor. If past experience is an indicator, you know you
will have nanoseconds to explain yourself. Your boss's ability to listen
lies somewhere between a rock and a two-by-four. You've packaged the
merits of your case into sound bites and rehearsed their delivery until
you find yourself mumbling them into the watercooler. In spite of your
preparation, intimidation rules. The moment you enter his office, your
personal power, your carefully rehearsed sound bites, and even self-
respect abandon you.

You feel as if you are on the floor and he is on a throne. An attempt
at chitchat is met with resounding silence. Before you know it, the clear
assertive reasoning you had intended cowers under his imposing asser-
tions. Your flurries of halfhearted, scattered "yeah, but" 's flit about like
leaves in the wind.

Gaining Home-Court Advantage

IMAGINE HOW DIFFERENT this could have been with the simple act of centering. Suppose you were able to show up at the door of his office as if you were approaching your own front door. Centered, clear, and composed you would be able to see him for what he is — just another fallible human being in the guise of your boss. This time you will pull the curtain on his manufactured tempest by waiting out his windy rhetoric, then calmly and clearly point out the merits of your performance.

And in the end? Who knows? It may be that your supervisor is flat-out intractable. The act of centering is not a magic pill that turns Mr. Potter into George Bailey. It does not promise to imbue you with the oratory skill of an Abe Lincoln. Nor will it guarantee happy endings.

But what it *will* do is improve the tactics you were otherwise planning. It will help you put your best foot forward, increasing the odds in your favor. No matter what the final outcome, centering gives you a home-court advantage, helping you make the best use of the resources available to you.

Centering, however, will only give you that advantage if you remember to do it. For most of us, it is not yet an ingrained behavior. Thus, despite the best intentions, the reality is that because it is not yet a habit we may very well forget to center, or remember after it is too late. Some say it takes twenty-one days of repetition to instill a habit. But how do you remember to cue into centering when it is still foreign? Set up trigger points.

Trigger points, like tying strings around fingers, are visual or situational reminders to begin practicing a new behavior. One way to do this with centering is first to isolate those distracting areas in your work life where a lack of centering has hurt most in the past. In our Mr. Potter episode above, for example, the boss's silence, the tone of his voice, and his demeanor were as distracting as those rocks I saw at the bottom of the cliff at Jackson Hole. What similar distractions can you isolate as trigger points to begin centering on the job tomorrow?

How to Make Centering a Habit

MENTALLY NOTE OR list a half dozen or so times in the last six months when centering would have given you the home-court advantage you lacked. Was there a certain someone or set of circumstances that made you particularly vulnerable to the "leaf in the wind" syndrome? Is there a pattern to these types of personalities or incidents? For example, did you lose your balance most often when you got pushed back regarding an idea? Was one particular coworker more apt to rattle your cage with some well-placed dig, always leaving you wondering what you could have said or done differently to defend yourself? Did you experience unwanted tension every time you went to a project review meeting?

If you can, tag just one particular individual or type of incident as a mental cue to kick in immediately with centering. Starting tomorrow and during these first few days, concentrate on perfecting centering with this one trigger point. After you've got that down, pick another and keep adding until you've mastered a number of different types of encounters and/or individuals. Other ideas to keep the centering habit a habit:

- Establish a "before the day begins" trigger point, like the closing door of the elevator that takes you to your office. As the door begins to close, reflexively begin to breath and find your center.

- Other such triggers might be the beeping sound of your car's infra-red key lock or your pressing the power button to start your computer.

Eventually you'll train yourself to start centering as soon as fretting rears its ugly head, right before an expected challenging situation, immediately after an intensive task, and before you walk through a door to attend a meeting. It will become as natural to you as flitting about in the wind used to be.

Pressure Cooker or Cooking under Pressure:
How Centering Made the Difference

HERE ARE TWO similar examples of giving a presentation under un-common pressure and how centering made a decided difference in the outcome.

Marilyn Thomas learned about centering techniques such as con-trolled breathing during the Lamaze classes she took in preparation for the birth of her child. She wishes she had known those skills before giving her first presentation as the newly appointed head of field oper-ations for a manufacturing firm, one of the most unnerving experiences of her life.

Marilyn had worked hard for weeks on her presentation, which was to be given during the annual sales meeting. It was the last one sched-uled for the week, forcing her to live with jitters during the entire con-vention. Finally her moment came. As the people filed into the conference room on Friday at four o'clock, she felt their restlessness. They had packing to do, planes to catch, and final good-byes to make. Many warned her as they arrived that they couldn't stay long. Instantly, the moment of glory she had hoped and meticulously planned for turned into a pressure cooker. She couldn't keep herself from being distracted by their fidgeting, glancing at watches, and the occasional defector sneaking out the back.

Then the professional woman's worst nightmare happened: she felt a hard burning lump gathering in her throat and her eyes welling up with tears. "I was quite young and inexperienced, facing down the barrels of a room full of well-seasoned men, some of whom I was sure had their doubts about my capabilities. This was my first chance to establish cred-ibility and I was about to lose it. I knew I had ten minutes at most with these guys to give a thirty-minute presentation. I found that by focusing exclusively on my most dramatic point, an entirely new way of inventory control that I had planned—not on the tears, not on who was leaving now—I was able to regain my composure. I blurted out the most salient points and before I had time to say, 'Thanks for coming,' they were out of there. The best I can say about that presentation is that I survived. When I think about what I know now, it makes me want to run back into that room and give it another shot just to see what a difference those centering skills can make."

I too faced a similarly challenging speaking engagement several years ago with the Young Presidents Organization (YPO). This group, let me tell you, is one of the toughest audiences a speaker can face. They are all presidents of their respective companies and are generally used to nothing but the best. If you don't captivate them in the first five minutes of your presentation, they won't hang around to be polite. They'll get up and leave just as Marilyn's audience did.

In addition to knowing this was a critical audience, I had serious butterflies for two other reasons. First, the subject of my workshop, "Re-spiriting the Workforce," was one most business leaders consider "soft." Second, this was the first time I had ever made such a presentation! No Off-Broadway for me. My debut was with the toughest audience around.

There is a saying about nervousness: "It's okay to have butterflies as long as they are flying in formation." Well, I had the butterflies, all right. The question I asked myself was how do I get them to fly in formation? The answer? You guessed it. Center. In the last minute be-fore I was introduced, I breathed deeply, consciously lowered my center of gravity, planted my feet solidly on the ground, and said a little prayer that what I had to offer would create "take-home value" for each person there. As I did this, a calm came over me and the butterflies started flying in formation. When they did, my nervous energy was transformed into a power source for my presentation. I was able to let go of my ego's need to look good or get high ratings and put my focus entirely on being of service to the people in the room.

By the time I was introduced, the teacher/presenter part of me was fully present and, no question, I was in the zone. Although I had pre-pared diligently and had carefully crafted notes, I barely glanced at them. It was as if something was being taught through me rather than by me. By the time the session ended, no one had left the room and the presentation received high marks. Thanks to my ability to center, I was able to transform a personally challenging situation into a big win for the YPOers in the room—and for me. Imagine how different Marilyn's experience would have been if she had had the ability to center before facing her antsy audience.

Stay Home

HOW DO YOU access your center? Simple. Practice. Then when you need to be home for an upcoming event, like the performance review described earlier or to handle an unanticipated tough situation like Marilyn's presentation, your ability to shift to this place of virtually boundless resource will be instantaneous and fluid.

Another way to stay home is to not wander too far or too often into the past or the future, but to learn to fully occupy each fleeting moment of the here and now.

BE PRESENT

When I'm with him I'm totally with him. I'm not where I've been or where I'm going. When I was a father, [although] I was with my kids [I was] usually somewhere else.

—RICHARD ATLAS,
speaking of his grandson

AUTHOR HUGH PRATHER said, "Deal with what is, not with what we want to be . . . because then, we spend effort on what isn't."[4] This is so true for many of us. There is little high quality of being when our thinking and talking are dominated by the past and the future to the point where there is no "is." How much better to focus only on those things we can influence and ignore those we can't because, as we all know, and too often forget, it is in the present where life happens. To paraphrase Woody Allen: "Eighty percent of life is just showing up."

The fact that focusing on the past and the future is actually required for productive and joyous living is not the issue. The problem is one of balance. Where we run into trouble is when past and future thinking squeezes the present right out of existence. When instead of learning from the past we fixate on it. When instead of anticipating the future we fret about it.

Being present requires more attentiveness than skill. To be successful, it is necessary to block out an unwanted focus on the past and the future, so that you can fully focus on the world of now.

Wanted Interruptions: *How to Stay in the Now*

AT LEAST FIVE times a day stop and check your verb tense. Are the words you use reflective of the past? Look for phrases such as "used to," "should have," "could have." The future will be described by words such as "ought to," "hope that," "going to," and "expect that." Also, to help you with your own awareness, notice the words those around you use. What verb tense signals their most predominant focus? By becoming quietly aware of the words of others, you will become more cognizant of your own.

Or ask someone to randomly interrupt your day and ask where your thinking is—in the past, present, or future? Make a note of where your concern was centered. Over time you will develop a pretty good reading of what tense you tend to dwell in. You can also create these "interruptions" by setting an alarm on a wristwatch or travel clock to remind you to do random checks.

Once you have developed this awareness, you can shift it. If you catch yourself focusing on the past or the future and would prefer to be in the present (remember past and future are not necessarily bad), gently reframe your thoughts, and focus on what is happening now.

Planning for the Present

PAST AND FUTURE thinking are obviously critical because, not only do they bring us the joy of memories and the excitement of hope, but they also inform the "now" with learning and potential. At a corporate level, for example, the process of creating a vision of the future can have a profound impact on the direction and success of an enterprise. Companies have spent billions on strategic planning processes that help them chart their futures and allocate resources. And the same is true on a personal level. We are well advised to make concrete plans for important life events like charting career changes, planning our retirement, or even arranging a vacation. When we "visualize" the future by imagining its ideal state as a present reality, we can plan accordingly. Without such attention to the future, certainly, we would be adrift with no clear direction and with random accomplishment.

On the other hand, although it is certainly wise to carry a spare tire in the trunk of your car, it's a huge waste of emotional energy to drive around fretting about getting a flat. Most of us don't go to such extremes, but many of us do routinely invest nervous energy in future events we can't control. Note the following true scenario:

RICHARD *(walking up to airline ticket counter)*: Hello, I'm checking in for the flight to Cincinnati.

KATE *(the ticket agent, big sigh)*: Could I see your ticket and a photo ID, please?

RICHARD *(smiling)*: Wow, that was a big sigh. Bad day?

KATE: Not yet, but there's a big snowstorm coming in and this place is going to be a zoo.

RICHARD: I see. So this is kind of an anticipatory funk, eh?

KATE *(smiling)*: Yeah. Thanks. The storm's not here yet, is it?

What was going on in this interaction is that, like many people, Kate was anticipating a future difficulty and reacting to it as if it had already happened, inducing unnecessary stress. For Kate, the fear of what *might* happen had the effect of producing almost the same anxiety as if it *had* happened. This was not only an unnecessary waste of emotion, it may have also deterred her ability to serve the customer in front of her at that precise moment. Her heavy sighing could have easily been misconstrued as her feelings for the customer, instead of the weather.

Put the Future Behind You with Actions Papers

WHAT VERB TENSE do you live in most of the time? Most of us live in the future tense (read worry). The positive side to future-think is when we wonder, dream, and plan. The negative side is when we dread and fret.

Write down the top three things that most often occupy your future thoughts. Are they positive or negative? If any is a negative, convert it to a positive by following these next steps for creating a positive outcome.

1. Identify a work outcome you would like to achieve. Write it on a piece of paper and describe it as if it were already accomplished. For example, "I have just completed the creation of a new expense management system for my department that saves money and time, and is well accepted by the staff." Write on the paper the date by which you will be able to make this statement a reality.

2. Keep that statement with you for 24 hours. Reread it at least five times.

3. On a separate piece of paper, list all the actions you will take to make your outcome a reality, and in what order they will occur.

4. Now, file your statement of outcome and don't look at it anymore.

You know what it is. Use your actions paper to dictate what you will actually do, starting with something today. Remember, if you simply do what is on this list, you will arrive at the outcome you desire. Just do what is on the list and don't worry about anything else.

Anticipating the Future: A *Two-Edged Sword*

SHARON IS A successful entrepreneur and, like most people who start their own business, is good at anticipating the future. When she is managing an important project she has an uncanny ability to anticipate what will go wrong. She sees pitfalls as clearly as if they were painted in pink Day-Glo and once she spots them she takes action to prevent them from happening. This talent is a two-edged sword, however.

On the other side of the sword, Sharon will imagine a future problem that doesn't exist and mentally make it a current reality and then worry and fret about it. Like Kate the airline representative, she expends precious time and energy focusing on something that hasn't happened and actually may never happen. When this takes place she is living the future today.

Like future thinking, past thinking can either benefit or detract, depending upon how much space we allow it to occupy in our lives. For most of us, experience *is* the best teacher. Whether bound in happy or painful memories, our past experiences can provide wise council. But too much preoccupation with the past can be a problem.

The "Present Moment" Technique

EVER WONDER WHY business draws so often upon sports for illumination of its principles? It's because they both involve games. They both require what sports psychologist Jim Loehr terms "mental toughness."[5] A big part of that toughness is the ability to stay in the present so that you can use all of your mental faculties to acutely listen, think, and do.

One on-the-fly technique athletes use to occupy the moment is called the "present moment technique."[6] Right after a screwup, or anytime you need to regain your composure, focus exclusively on the present act of breathing until you are back in control and fully able to occupy the moment. Here's how:

1. Take a really deep belly breath (as described on page 52).
2. Hold it for one to five seconds.
3. Exhale slowly, all the while focusing on how your body is relaxing and letting go of tension.
4. Repeat.

Why don't you try it right now?

Putting the Present into a Timeline

IN HIS BOOK *Breakpoint and Beyond,* George Land notes that the typical growth pattern of organizations parallels that of individuals and can be described as an S curve. The figure below is an adaptation of Land's original model, which indicates the three stages of growth: Survival, Success, and Grow or Die. In the Survival stage, you're scrambling to get a toehold. For a company, that means people are highly motivated and customer-focused because in order to survive the organization needs to get customers. The entrepreneurial energy is electric. All members of the organization are in the same boat working together and rowing as hard as they can. The company is quick and adaptable to the slightest change in its operating environment. In this stage the words "It's not my job" are never heard.

If the company makes it through the Survival stage, and most don't, it begins to experience some success. The market responds well and customer relationships begin to multiply. Growth is rapid and profits abound. The key in this phase is to figure out the basis for the success and lock it in to everything the organization does. It's as if there are a

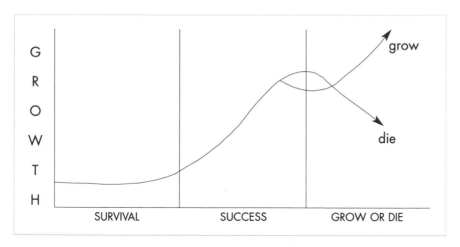

few key levers that, when pulled, create the desired success. Once these levers are identified, the organization focuses all its energy into making sure those levers are the only ones being pulled. It hires, trains, and promotes the best lever pullers for those particular levers. It institutes a bureaucracy of inflexible policies and procedures that will ensure optimal pulling of those precise levers. The company has found the success formula and, by gosh, nothing will deter it from sticking to that exact prescription for success.

The moment of truth comes as the organization passes to the third stage, Grow or Die. As you can see from the curve, as a company comes out of the Success stage it will either reinvent itself or slip into a downward spiral that inexorably leads to its demise. One only needs to look at companies like Pan Am, Wang, and Digital to understand this phenomenon. The problem here is that market conditions change and the Second Stage organization is so preoccupied with pulling its levers, it doesn't realize that the new game is about pushing buttons. Sadly, as the levers become attached to nothing and the market starts slipping away, the company frantically and futilely pulls them harder and faster.

The lesson here is that though it is instructive, useful, and often pleasurable to revisit the past or venture into the future, it is only a focus on the present that enables us to fill each minute with what Rudyard Kipling called "sixty-seconds' worth of distance run" in his classic poem, "If." Removing those tensions of tenses conserves our energy and focuses it like a laser beam on what is needed right now to fully appreciate the present and get where we want to go.

Your Career's Timeline

Think of the S curve as a model for your career. Plot the course of the shifts your career have taken over the years.

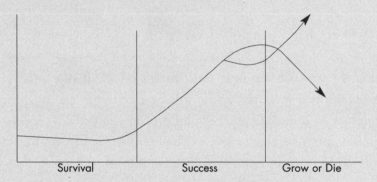

| Survival | Success | Grow or Die |

Place an "N" where you are right now. What are the implications of being there? If you are in the declining phase, ask yourself:

1. To what extent are you willing to learn from, but also let go of, the past?

2. Are you doggedly pulling the same old levers—levers that may not be attached to anything worthwhile?

3. AFL-CIO president Lane Kirkland said, "Those who do remember the past may not know when it is over."[7] Is this fatal preoccupation with *what was*, true of where you are right now?

Staying in the Present Is a Performance Issue

Life is difficult? Nah. Life is easy. Self-help books are easy. Golf—now, golf is difficult.

—JOHN SKOW,
journalist[8]

H. L. MENCKEN once said that "golf ruins a good walk." For those of you who agree, who think golf is silly, well, I guess the idea of grown men and women spending five hours wandering around acres of manicured grass, trying to put a little white ball into a hole the size of a teacup, can be difficult to understand. Unless you play. Then, of course, you get it. For many of us it's full of metaphors and insights into the game of life.

For example, after a remarkable string of victories on the Professional Golfers Association (PGA) tour a couple of years ago, Peter Jacobson was asked what accounted for his sudden success. He attributed it to improved putting. No longer was he focusing on getting the ball in the cup, but rather on perfecting the stroke itself so that "the cup would get in the way of the ball." Jacobson had disciplined himself to worry only about how to shut down the oppressive tension of tenses, past and future, and zero in on the now. Conversely, listen to the kind of self-talk your average Saturday morning golfer goes through in preparing to putt.

Okay, only a six-footer. If I sink this I'll get a par and, depending on what Bert does, probably win the hole for our team . . . that'll put us up, hmm, three with four holes to play. . . . (Future)

Meanwhile, as our golfer stalks the putt, sizes it up from every angle and tries a couple of practice swings, the self-talk continues:

I had a putt just like this on the sixth hole. . . . Missed it because I didn't follow through. (Past)

At this point, our golfer makes the stroke. More times than not the "hole misses the ball" because the golfer is *everywhere but the present*. Whether it's golf or any other sport, business, volunteer work, or simply washing your car, the undeniable fact is that *today's performance must be achieved today*—now. It can't be achieved yesterday or tomorrow. When we live in the moment, when we concentrate on the present act of striking the ball correctly or serving the customer or trying to improve employee performance, then our chances of finding the hole, the sale, or better performances are greatly enhanced.

Making Time Stand Still with Meditation

IT'S 4:22 IN the morning and Moses Joseph, CEO of B-Tree Systems, has already been up and at 'em for seven minutes. "If I dawdle, I'm lost," he explains. "I want to feel as if I'm on top of the day, rather than have the day control me. I mount a mental attack on time from the first minute on." And part of his mental attack includes taking ten minutes to meditate.

So why does Joseph meditate first thing in the morning after he's just had a night's rest? Because even while sleeping the mind never stops. Like sleep for the body, Joseph starts every day by resting and rejuvenating his mind through this time-proven method of learning to be present: "I'll make good decisions . . . because I'm tuned to everything that's going on."⁹

The hardest part about meditation is finding the time to do it. Meditation is great any time you need to get back to the "now." Starting your morning with it, however, ensures that it will be done at least once and also sets an ever "present" tone to the entire day. So how do you meditate?

According to Jon Kabat-Zinn: "*Meditation is simplicity itself. . . . It's about stopping and being present, that is all.*"¹⁰ For the beginner it is nothing more than deep relaxation, during which your brain waves slow from your normal waking existence (beta state) to a slower, more relaxed (alpha) state. Here's how to shift states.

1. Find a place that is quiet and free from distractions and get comfortable.
2. Close your eyes and take several deep breaths. Continue to breathe slowly and deeply.
3. Let your mind relax and focus on a single word, a number or an imaginary design. As thoughts of the events of the day or future tasks creep in, simply usher them out of your consciousness. You might imagine a sound-proof room where they can go and make all the noise they want.

DETACH FROM OUTCOMES

The law of detachment says that in order to acquire anything in the physical universe, you have to relinquish your attachment to it. This doesn't mean you give up the intention to create your desire. You don't give up your attachment to the results.

DEEPAK CHOPRA,
The Seven Spiritual Laws of Success

TO SAY THAT Commander D. Michael Abrashoff was a successful leader while in charge of the U.S. Navy's $1 billion warship, the USS *Benfold,* is an understatement. He was nothing short of a miracle worker. According to *Fast Company* magazine, in 1998 he gave the navy back "$600,000 of its $2.4 million maintenance budget and $800,000 of its $3 million repair budget"—an absolutely unheard of gesture for a ship commander or any other government worker, for that matter. Even businesspeople would be reluctant to do so. His ship had the lowest incidences of "mission degrading" equipment failure and the highest gunnery score in the Pacific. He cut the time required for predeployment training in port from twenty-two days to five. The *Benfold*'s combat readiness earned the coveted Spokane Trophy, an award that a warship in this class hadn't won in ten years or more.

A Captain Bligh? Hardly. Fifty-four percent of career sailors quit the navy after two tours of duty, but not Abrashoff's crew. An astonishing 100 percent of his sailors remained onboard for at least one more turn. Talk about employee retention. The fact that his sailors loved him — loved the way he sent the cooks to culinary school; the way he found a way to give them two weekends off a month instead of the usual one; the way he enlisted their talents as well as their time through "aggressive listening" — was more than just heartwarming. His retention rate saved the navy $1.6 million in retraining and miscellaneous personnel costs in a single year and the battle readiness of the *Benfold* made it the ship of choice for the most dangerous and challenging Gulf War missions.

So what is his secret? He's got a lot of them, but basically they all boil down to this: "All I ever wanted to do in the navy was command a ship. I don't care if I ever get promoted again. And that attitude has enabled me to do the right things for my people instead of doing the right things for my career."[11]

Ironically, it was Abrashoff's ability to detach from the pressures of his career, caring less about promotion and more about doing things right, which ultimately ended up securing his promotion.

The Outcomes-Oriented Business Culture

DETACHING FROM OUTCOMES, as illustrated above, can be an extraordinarily powerful way to get back home to that zone of almost unconscious high performance *and* peace. However, of the three roads I recommend — centering, be present, detach from outcomes — this one is the most difficult to achieve. It requires that we step back from what we desire most — results.

In today's highly performance-oriented business culture, attachment to results is more than just powerful. It is self-defining. Too often I see people routinely confuse their self-worth with their ability to "make the numbers," even when in many cases these numbers are unachievable. This "I-am-my-numbers" attitude can be devastating to your self-image. I know one business leader who positively soars when she makes her quarterly targets but slumps into a gray funk and thinks of herself as unworthy when she misses.

I remember a Little League game I attended where angry parents shouted criticisms and insults at the coach. Why? Not because of his relationship with the kids who played for him, which was outstanding, but because of his team's mediocre won-lost record. That mediocre record, by the way, was the result of his trying to play everybody — even clumsy little right-fielder Billy Bumble who couldn't catch a baseball in a peach basket.

Perhaps the words spoken in the sixties by a tyrannical, egocentric, and undeniably brilliant football coach has helped to transform the national psyche. "Winning isn't everything," growled Green Bay Packers' Vince Lombardi, "it's the only thing." That attitude, tolerant only of perfection, dehumanizes those who strive but fail to win a championship. Although a total emphasis on winning is curiously seductive, it can be damaging in the long run.

Business Leads the Way

IN BUSINESS THIS outcome mania is exacerbated by Wall Street's obsessive preoccupation with quarterly earnings and our constant monitoring of results. "Management by objectives," "key result achievement," "key job requirements," and other such initiatives have become the cornerstone of management practices around the world. Cascading down from them are a substrata of strategic imperatives, milestones, benchmarks, interim reports, objectives, key result areas, targets, and expected outcomes. Our world has become burdened with new and different ways of establishing desired results and creating sophisticated systems for measuring progress against them. Such compulsive tracking seems to reflect a belief that if we don't continually check on how we are doing, we will somehow lose our capacity to do it.

The Relationship between Goals and Results

DOES THIS MEAN I'm against having goals? Of course not. *I believe that the creation of performance targets and methods for measuring progress against them is critical to the success of any organization or individual.* Many of us seem to have grown up with the notion that the more we emphasize results, the more results we will get. This belief is represented by the straight diagonal line on the following chart.

Based on the work of Harvard psychologist David McClelland, in reality the performance curve looks more like a bell curve.[12] Results actually deteriorate when there is *too little* emphasis on them. When this happens, people have no direction and become confused. If the organization thrives, it is more by *chance* than direction. Too much emphasis on results, however, creates stress and *chokes* the performer. It is a moderate emphasis on results that creates the *challenge* that stimulates people to high performance.

Stop now and think of the implications of setting an objective and then continually harping on performance against that objective as a means of motivating workers. Remember in the golf putting analogy how the past or future gets in the way of today's performance? Well, if I am your manager and every day I remind you how far behind your numbers you are, what am I doing? I am taking you right out of the present, where you have to perform today, and pushing you into the future. In the great majority of cases it is a negative or, at best, useless management intervention because you are already aware of the gap. I

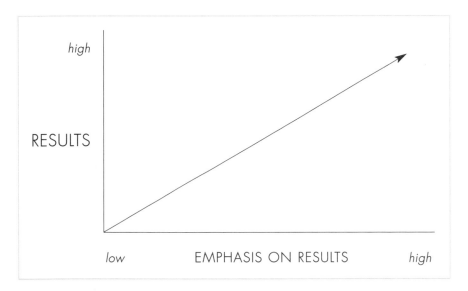

suspect that in all too many cases this happens because jawboning about goals makes the manager feel (1) better and (2) in control. But what it really does is diminish the performer's capacity to succeed.

Focus on the Leading Indicators

IT FOLLOWS, OF course, that if this obsession with outcomes affects the individual performer—and it does—it will then affect the overall success of the company. Ironically, the company that focuses its energy and measurement exclusively on bottom-line profit is the one least likely to achieve that goal. Here's why: a company's profit is a lagging indicator. It, and the resulting earnings per share, are the last figures you can calculate. That's why they call it "the bottom line." By the time you calculate it, the game is over. You are just looking at the scoreboard. With today's rapidly changing times, managing by a lagging indicator will ultimately create disappointing results and even outright failure. It is like steering a sailboat through dangerous reefs by facing aft and looking at the vessel's wake.

Outcomes Fixation = Performance Vexation

Here's how to chart your on-the-job performance in the face of pressure to produce. List three outcomes on which you are fixated. Are you expected to turn around a project, say, 30% faster this month? Are you hoping to beat last year's sales results by 15%? Are you looking for ways to reduce production defects by .5% in the next quarter? Are you striving to decrease phone time with each customer by an average of 30 seconds? Whatever your outcome goals, list them here:

Outcome #1: ....
Outcome #2: ....
Outcome #3: ....

Now, on the chart below, plot each of those outcomes relative to the pressure you are feeling to hit the targets.

Fixation on Outcomes

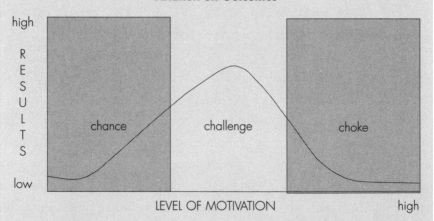

If you placed an outcome in the shaded zone to the left (chance), then you need to develop more intensity around the result. If you have trouble doing this, reassess the result. It may be less important than you think.

If, however, you put a number in the shaded area to the right (choke) you may be too compulsive about achieving that result. You might want to think about whether you are getting pushed into "future thinking." What is keeping you so focused on the outcome? How can you back off a little and put your focus on what you have to do today in order to achieve the outcome you desire? (Challenge)

So what are the lagging indicators for your career? Clearly there are three: salary, promotion, and performance ratings. Each of these usually reflects the aggregate of your past performance, and relying on them as a current scorecard may lull you into a false sense of security.

Astute performers will find and manage the *leading* indicators. In their pioneering work on the balanced business scorecard, Robert Kaplan and David Norton point out three indicators: customer satisfaction, quality output, and employee morale. These three leading indicators are just as applicable to your job as they are to a business, because in this new world of work, nothing is permanent or secure, including your job. You're in competition with other employees, "reductions in staff," and potentially, outside vendors who might do what you do better and cheaper. In reality, we've become free agents, self-employed.

The 3 Leading Indicators:
A Personal Performance Review

Create your own personalized version of the balanced business scorecard by indicating where you are gaining or faltering in the areas that matter most.

How do these three leading indicators apply to your personal work? The customer in customer satisfaction does not necessarily mean the final user of your product or service. For our purposes, it simply means anyone who receives your work, whether a manager, coworker, or an actual customer. "Product quality" simply means the effectiveness and efficiency with which you do your work as judged by your customers. Your product quality might be how well you keep your boss's business life orderly with a system that anticipates her needs and   keeps her external customers satisfied with a pleasant phone voice and accommodating manner.

And employee morale? The employee here is *you.* If you aren't jazzed about your work or performance—as indicated by your attitude, your ability to actively listen, and your eagerness to serve—then nobody else is going to be. (We hope that after you've finished this book, you'll be able to put a "5" in the boxes below.)

Say you are in charge of rolling out a media relations campaign for a new product and your responsibilities include coordinating strategy meetings, forecasting costs, debriefing product managers, and preparing press releases. You would list those responsibilities below and then, using a scale from 1 to 5 (5 being stellar achievement), rate the three leading indicators for each area. Similarly, break down what you do into specific areas of responsibility and rate them to see where you've got it together and where you need improvement. Finally, add the three scores to derive your overall on-the-job performance. Where are you doing well? What areas need your attention?

Area of Responsibility	Customer Satisfaction	Product Quality	My Morale	Total Score

When Outcomes Get in the Way

ON A PERSONAL level, a compulsion with results can thwart the desired outcome. A study of world-class athletes revealed that the more
they fixated on the *outcome*, winning, the less likely they were to win.
In fact, a single-minded preoccupation with winning an Olympic gold
medal, accompanied by the tremendous pressure this generates, can
become a huge psychological barrier to victory. At the 1998 Winter
Olympics in Nagano, Japan, Tara Lipinski, less preoccupied with the
Gold than favored Michelle Kwan, let it flow. After winning the top
prize, she said, "I didn't think about winning. I didn't think about
beating anyone. I just thought about going out there and having a
great time. . . . I felt I knew what the Olympics was about. Pure joy.
And I put it into my program."[13]

This phenomenon was reported by sports psychologist Shanc Murphy
in a *Business Week* article entitled "Zen and the Art of Olympic Success." Wrote Murphy: "Any time you get into that state where you're
thinking about the result instead of what you're doing, you're pretty
much screwed—to use the scientific term."[14]

Results and Expectations

EXPECTATIONS ARE RESULTS in action. Our bosses, teachers, and
friends have expectations for us, and of course we have them for ourselves. What it all adds up to is that—whatever the source—we are
"expected" to do or achieve certain things. As helpful and powerful as
expectations can be, they can also be limiting, even debilitating. One
form of detaching from outcomes, then, is to let go of your expectations.
A scary thought for some, I am sure.

In her book *The Centered Skier*, Denise McCluggage makes a per-
suasive argument against having expectations. She describes a Friday
night meeting with skiers who have enrolled in her weekend class.

To start the meeting she has them think of any expectations they have for the weekend and then, on an imaginary piece of paper, write them down. She then asks the wannabe skiers to crumble the paper and throw it in an imaginary bonfire in the center of the room. With this done, she goes on to explain how expectations can, after all, be limiting:

> Expectations are the surest road to disappointment. For instance, if you have arrived Friday night in a gentle piling of new snow and you awake Saturday morning to a shroud of fog and the distant sound of dripping, you are disappointed.
>
> You are now faced with two immediate choices. Stay disappointed . . . or recognize that it is your attachment to your expectation, to what you wished for, that has soured your view of the world. . . . Your disappointment will only feed your insistence on being disappointed. It will only underscore the contrast between the day you had in mind and the day that is — the contrast between desire and reality.

Whenever I find myself hugely disappointed in anything, I check in to see what my expectations were. As in the scenario above, nine times out of ten it was my expectations that caused the problem.

Does this mean that the pleasure of anticipating the closing of an important business deal or realizing 100 percent of a potential bonus gets put in the Dumpster?

Of course not. But when your prospect postpones the buying decision or you fall 5 percent short of the expected bonus and you're upset, take a moment to realize that just maybe it's your expectations that are causing the problem. They can be altered — or dropped. Often such problems actually bring us unexpected gifts. Or as Denise says to her skiers, "Why go home with a perfect right turn when you might go home knowing how to fly?"

Rewired Outcomes

BECAUSE MOST OF us grow up as children dreaming about what we wish for and want, over time we are naturally conditioned to let our lives be governed by attachments to such things. To counterbalance this and detach from the emotional dependence on these outcomes, we can "rewire" ourselves. This can be achieved by the retraining exercise described below:

1. In your daily life, notice when you are disappointed at not having things turn out as you wanted or expected them to. These need not be big life events and, in fact, will work better with small disappointments. You were planning to have lunch with a coworker you rarely see, for example, and are looking forward to it. An hour before the scheduled lunch, she calls and has to cancel. You are disappointed. Or perhaps you have been called into your manager's office and are told your pet project has been denied budget approval.

2. Think of three reasons why whatever happened could actually be a good thing? Perhaps the canceled lunch allowed you more time to polish an important business plan. Perhaps your pet project was premature and pushing for it again later may mean it will have the full backing it needs and deserves.

With realizations such as these you learn how to put less inappropriate emotional investment in specific results.

Attachment to Inputs

IF YOU DON'T attach to expectations or outcomes, what do you attach to? Inputs. Life and career coach Joanne Brem, formerly in large-systems sales at the high-tech giant Amdahl, can personally testify to the effectiveness of keeping your focus entirely on inputs—on the things you do to prepare for a result—and off the desired outcome itself. The accolades Brem amassed while at Amdahl were nothing short of startling. Her first year out as an account executive—as the third woman, and the youngest, ever to hold this position—she won the western region "Rookie of the Year" award. Brem continued to set sales records, earning numerous awards, including repeatedly winning Amdahl's highest for sales. In one year alone, Brem was responsible for more than $30 million in sales. Talk about outcomes.

Yet, here's what Brem said to herself before each call: "Whether I make this sale or not will not even be a footnote on my epitaph." Sound like she didn't care about the sale? Not at all! She did everything in her power to ensure it. "I did my homework. I kept note pads by my bed, in the car, everywhere, just in case I needed to capture a sudden insight or strategy. I ran through every question customers might have, and even more important, the ones they might not. I woke up in the middle of the night thinking about them. I cared very much about the sale, but my career took off once I got this truth deep in my bones: You have to let it go."

This truth came to Brem after a difficult dry spell that lasted over a year and it immediately sparked four straight years of top sales performance. Says Brem, "Instead of worrying about my quota, I focused on helping my customers. I found that by doing everything in my power to satisfy their needs—*and* totally trusting that the best outcome would result—ironically also maximized my access to it. It unleashed my highest levels of listening, openness, being in the present, creativity, and spontaneity . . . and customers sensed it. Because they sensed it—sensed that I was wholly there for *them* and not for the sale—they trusted me. Once that happened, the orders just took care of themselves."

Detaching from outcomes is contrary to the way we are managed, the way many of us were brought up, and, for some of us, contrary to our nature. In the Western world, a fixation on results is tattooed into our psyches as indelibly as hieroglyphics on the Great Pyramid. This bias is very difficult to shift, but when you detach from burdensome outcomes, not only will you find yourself achieving the results you have separated from, your entire life will be graced by more ease, less worry, and more space and time in which to simply laugh and enjoy yourself and your work.

CENTERED, PRESENT, DETACHED . . . HOME AT LAST

TO INTEGRATE THE business and personal aspects of these "be home" ideas, imagine the following scenario. You are selling office supplies for a large firm and are part of a 300-person sales force. There are three weeks left in the last month of the last quarter and you are in real danger of not making your sales quota. Your manager has just had a serious talk with you, reminding you that if you don't rack up pretty spectacular orders between now and the end of the month, you will miss the quota for sure.

He points out that there is a lot riding on being over your quota: a bonus, extra commission, a trip to Hawaii with your spouse as a member of the One Hundred Percent Club, the prestige and esteem of your workmates, and possibly future promotion. In fact, there is so much riding on this month's production, and so much stress because of it, that after the meeting you have trouble sleeping at night.

You have a limited amount of prime selling time left, which means every call has to count. It is Thursday and you have set up a call with the office manager of a medium-size company. As you pull into the visitor's parking space, you mentally review the nine or ten most likely reasons this person should buy your products. Your goal? To get back in your car in an hour with a signed order in your hand. As you are escorted into the customer's office, you mentally review the tried-and-true closing techniques that have worked for you with other customers. You are introduced, shake hands, and stalk the order from that moment on.

After working with thousands of salespeople in hundreds of different organizations around the world, I can tell you that this is not an uncommon scenario. What is wrong with it? The customer is simply not factored into the equation. Other than someone who signs an order, he or she is not a major consideration. What is the major consideration? *You* getting *your* order so *you* can make *your* quota. And who's to blame you?

The management pressure, payoffs, incentives, and frequent reports reminding you how far behind you are constitute the trap. They force you to obsess about the outcome, which takes you out of the present, which keeps you from getting into the flow, which keeps you from focusing on the customer, which keeps you from understanding his or her true needs, which keeps you from addressing those needs, which ultimately keeps you from getting the order.

Again, not for a minute am I saying that results are not important. They are. But when they become so huge in your psyche as to eclipse all reasonable performance, they have become dysfunctional.

An alternative scenario to the one above would be for you, the office products salesperson, to note the gap between your current and desired performance, acknowledge the importance of exceeding the quota, and then detach from the outcome. How? By developing a specific plan to close the gap and then execute the plan in the here and now, with power and discipline. Other than acting in the present to close it, you don't waste an erg of energy fretting about the gap itself. This would be akin to driving around worrying that with each turn of your tire it might go flat.

And where does centering come in? Well, the first time it would come in handy would be before that pep talk from your manager. And how about taking a moment to center yourself before walking into a prospect's office?

While you're at it, why not make the purpose of every call to add value to the customer in that moment, whether or not you walk out with an order? If you get in the habit of creating such value, customers will always want to spend time with you, and, like Joanne Brem, more often than not you will end up with the order you wanted in the first place.

The above scenario is applicable to every situation and every occupation. As you begin respiriting your work life by being centered, present, and detached from outcomes, good things will begin to happen. You will, in the words of the nineteenth-century Anglican preacher Frederick W. Robertson, "tear off that mask of guarded and suspicious coldness, which the world forces us to wear in self-defense" and go home to "the place of confidence." When you work with confidence, groundedness, and clarity, your work—whether handling administrative tasks, working on the production line, delivering packages, selling, serving customers, or whatever—*and* your work life can be transformed to a place where you not only get what you want but enjoy the process of getting it.

So where do you go from here? How can you begin respiriting your work life right now? You have already begun. For some of you, this may have been the first time you've thought seriously about these three ways of *being home*. Now, whenever you are in a situation that requires you to center, be present, or detach from outcomes, perhaps these words will come to mind.

Even greater benefit can be derived, however, if you develop your capacity to remain at home. The best way to accomplish this is to train yourself. Practicing the previous exercises and techniques will help you learn how to extend your ability to be home from a sometime thing to an ever-present way of being. When you have achieved this you will have greatly enhanced not only your work life but your entire life as well.

Action Steps

ONE WAY TO move from intention to action is to decide what steps you will actually begin to take to stay home. Based on the work you've

already completed in this chapter and any helpful information you may
have read, complete the following:

- • I will start . . .

- • I will stop . . .

- • I will do more . . .

- • I will do less . . .

- • I will do differently . . .

Create Your Own Reality

The greatest discovery of my generation is that a human being can alter his life by altering his attitude.

— WILLIAM JAMES

SOME TIME AGO I had lunch with Bill, a sales representative for a chemical company, and started the conversation with the conventional, "How ya doing?" Bill's answer was short and emphatic: "Terrible!" Unable to miss the pain and frustration in that response, I probed deeper, "What's up?"

"Well, this morning I overslept because my alarm clock broke. Then as I was rushing to an appointment with an important customer, I got a flat tire. Of course, it was raining and in the process of changing the flat, I ruined my new dress shoes. When I finally got to the customer's office it was too late. He was tied up in another meeting and couldn't see me. To top it off, when I got back to the office my boss, who is pretty much out of it anyway, started nagging me about some petty administrative thing that didn't matter. So if you ask me how I'm doing the answer is pretty easy: Terrible!"

To be sure Bill wasn't having a great day. We can all relate. Whether we like it or not, as we live from day to day, we are going to be beset by events and circumstances that we did not expect or want in our lives. Whether it's fate, karma, or simply the whim of the universe, we will continually be confronted by intrusions that are beyond our control: oversleeping because of a broken alarm clock, a flat tire at the worst possible moment, a boss who flies off the handle over nothing. These daily events are out of our control. While we really don't have much to say about unwanted intrusions, we can have control over their effect on us.

REALITY IS A CHOICE

MANY OF US give away our power over these unwanted interruptions because we label them "misfortunes" and, like the *Road Runner* cartoon character, we freeze in the middle of the road as a Mack truck of sadness, panic, frustration, or rage steamrolls us flat as a pancake. Although it might start this way, it doesn't have to stay this way. Adversity and daily troubles only have the power to crush us if we give our permission. As Franklin Delano Roosevelt put it so well: "Men are not prisoners of fate, but only prisoners of their own minds."

The ensuing dialogue between Bill and me makes this clearer.

"Wow, Bill, the day isn't half over and you've already had your share of nasty surprises."

"You bet I have," responded Bill, still frowning.

"Let me ask you something," I said. "When you say that you are terrible, who is actually deciding you *are* terrible?"

Bill looked a little puzzled before he answered, "I guess I am."

"Well, you seem to have some choice here, so why are you choosing to be terrible?"

Bill responded with a twinge of anxiety. "I don't know. It was just kind of automatic."

I persisted, "As long as you are deciding, do you think it would be possible or even conceivable to decide anything else?"

Beginning to get my point, Bill grudgingly said, "Yeah. As long as I'm deciding I guess I can decide to feel any way I want to about it. I could even laugh it off and find some humor in it, couldn't I?"

The point here is important and simple. We don't have a lot to say about many of the things fate throws our way, but, at the end of the day, *we have everything to say about how we react to them*. In effect, after we discharge whatever instantaneous emotional reaction may accompany an unpleasant event, we don't have to remain mired in that emotion. Rather, we can choose to create our own reality around these events by simply interpreting them differently.

What's Worked Before

TAKE A MOMENT and reflect on your career . . .

1. Think of a time in your career when you got stuck by letting your attitude toward events diminish your effectiveness.
2. What did you do to restore your productivity?
3. Was there a time when you felt as though your career was hampered by something, only to realize later on that it was the very thing that ultimately furthered your career?

Creating a New Reality on a Grand Scale: *From Ten Minutes of Despair to New Dreams*

AUTHOR HUGH PRATHER asks: "There is a me that curses and struggles and one that walks in peace. Do I have a choice of selves?"[1] The answer is a resounding "Yes!" Every day we ourselves are the mitigating factor in the joy and satisfaction we experience, whether overcoming the common tensions and frustrations that can litter our workday, if we let them, or overcoming the lifetime effects of a tragedy. The question isn't whether or not you will get hurt, the question is whether you will choose to suffer. In short, do you see yourself as a victim or a survivor?

Ted Henter is a survivor.

It took Henter, a mechanical engineer, ten minutes to discharge his emotion of despair at being blinded in a car accident. "I was a sighted kid. I grew up with dreams. But once I was blinded, none of those were relevant anymore. I had to think up new dreams. So I had . . . ten minutes of despair. I knew that what happened to me was for my own good . . . something good was gonna come out of it."[2]

What came out of it was JAWS (Job Access With Speech), a computer screen reader developed by Henter that opened a world of job and educational opportunities for the blind.[3] There's a chance that when you call FedEx, AT&T, Honeywell, Marriott, or a growing number of Fortune 500 companies, your service rep might be a blind person using a JAWS-adapted computer to help you.

Once Henter saw his dreams destroyed, he took control back by creating new ones, ideas that took advantage of his adversity. He saw limited opportunity for a blind mechanical engineer and went back to school to learn computers. One thing led to another and now blinded people, who have a notoriously low level of employment, have greater opportunity. Indeed Henter's prophecy that "something good" was going to come out of tragedy was self-fulfilling. He made it happen. He determined the reality that would result. He chose not to remain a victim of tragedy but to take advantage of it for his own purposes, to create and fulfill new dreams.

Creating a New Reality Day to Day

HENTER'S LIFE MAY have changed dramatically, but he is still the same person at his core. Henter was a motorcycle-racing champion before he was blinded, and today he is a blind waterskiing champion. His competitive spirit remains, albeit in a different sport. According to resiliency expert Al Siebert, people "handle disastrous crises in the same way they handle everyday life."[4]

Every common daily struggle — the petty personality conflict, the policy tug-of-war, the process snafu — is preparing you to handle the really big events, like being passed over for a promotion, losing your job, or facing a transfer. Those larger events just magnify your core habits of perception and reaction, whether they are positive or negative, whether as passive victim or as active learner. The converse is equally true. If you believe a big positive change in your situation — a promotion, a raise, a new boss — is going to drastically and permanently make you happy at work, think again. Aristotle said: "We are what we repeatedly do. Excellence, then, is not an act, but a habit." The same applies to happiness. We are happy if we habitually perceive things in the best possible light and habitually train ourselves to look for the positive, to view every occurrence as a chance for growth and good.

Choosing Your Happiness

SOMEONE WINS A major contract that lands him in a corner office. Someone else is pink-slipped. Guess who ends up happier a year later? Believe it or not, it is impossible to predict. Why? Because though events in our lives spike highs and lows, we quickly return to what our predilection for happiness was before the events occurred. The fact is, one year later, even lottery winners as a group are just about as happy, or unhappy, as they were before the windfall.[5] An angry person who wins the contract, promotion, or the lottery might ride euphoric for a while, but chances are he or she will still end up an angry person.

Forget about that hoped-for raise buying long-term happiness. If money bought happiness, the super-rich would be super-happy. But they're not. A *Forbes* magazine article, "Does Money Buy Happiness?" cites a study that found that the super-rich scored only slightly above average happiness: 5.82, on a scale from 1 to 10, 1 being the least happiest. The regular wage earner scored around 5.34. In fact, one-third of those money-magnets were less happy than regular earners. This is why one of the wealthiest people on earth, investment guru Warren Buffet, warns against thinking that a lot of money is going to change you for the better. "If you were a jerk before, you'll be a bigger jerk with a billion dollars."[6]

If a happier reality at work isn't about money, what is it about? Surprisingly, factors like sex, race, and age have little or no statistical bearing on perceived levels of happiness.[7] It does have something to do with whether or not good or bad things happen to you, but only in the short term—usually about three months of pain or pleasure after a major event.[8]

According to studies by psychologists Ed Diener and David Myers, there are four reliable predictors of happiness: self-esteem, optimism, being an extrovert, and a feeling of control.[9] Notice that each of these four happiness factors is rooted in what *you do*, what *you think*, and who *you are* at your core, and not a single one relates to what is done to you, or how others think of you.

These predictors reflect how we internally process the things that have happened to us, are happening to us, and will happen to us. So how can you create a reality in every sense and every tense—of the future, the past, and the present—in a way that serves you best? Let's look at three traits of resilient performers to see how adversity, as well as common daily frustrations, can be used as tools to create the reality you want at work. They are:

1. Be an optimist.
2. Transform adversity into advantage.
3. Create a positive life story.

Happiness at work comes to people who, by mastering their thoughts and actions, bend circumstances to fit their will and find the reality they wish for. This reality not only directly affects daily job satisfaction but ultimately affects career success. This is so because, in the end, it's how we deal with the tough things at work—how, by our example, we inspire others to transform difficulties, to stay motivated and resilient, to find happiness and joy in the midst of trials—that affects the course of our career far more than how we handle the easy things.

How Have You Recovered from Adversity?

1. Think of a time when unexpected adversity barged into your work life and threw you significantly off track. This was a clear setback that kept you down for more time than you would have liked.

2. Think of a time when you encountered a similar setback, licked your wounds for a bit and then bounced back. What was it that enabled you to find the resilience to recover from the one and get bogged down by the other?

3. Based on this analysis, what are two or three actions you can take to recover from and turn a negative event into a positive outcome?

BE AN OPTIMIST

Most people are as happy as they make up their minds to be.

—ABRAHAM LINCOLN

IF OPTIMISM WAS available by prescription, it would be considered a miracle drug. Research on optimism's effect on health has shown that it alleviates depression, reduces the chances of getting sick, enhances the immune system, lowers stress, stalls the onset and progress of diseases, reduces the risk of accidents and violence, and even measurably increases the bounce in your step. Moderately optimistic people tend to live an average twelve years longer than moderately negative people.[10] That fact should be enough to make a Norman Vincent Peale out of anyone.

But there's more. Research proves that optimistic people are more productive, more likely to be promoted, and make more money. They are able to stay with difficult tasks long after others have given up, find jobs faster than their less upbeat counterparts, and have more satisfying interpersonal relationships.

As we know from the research cited above, an optimistic attitude doesn't just make us feel better emotionally, it also materially changes our circumstances for the better—professionally, personally, and physically.[11] In fact, optimistic thinking can literally save your life. Just ask Jerry.

You can find Jerry's entire story, "Attitude Is Everything" by Francie Baltazar-Schwartz, in Jack Canfield's *Chicken Soup for the Soul at Work*. Here is an abbreviated version.[12] Jerry—according to the author and former coworker—was "the kind of guy you loved to hate. He was always in a good mood and always had something positive to say. If someone would ask him how he was doing, he would reply, 'If I were any better, I'd be twins!' "

The story goes on to recount how Jerry was a unique restaurant manager because his waiters would follow him to whatever restaurant he was working for at the time. They followed Jerry because of his attitude, which he sums up this way:

Life is all about choices. You choose how you react to situations. You choose how people will affect your mood. You choose to be in a good mood or a bad mood. The bottom line: it's your choice how you live life.

Early one morning while working, three robbers held up Jerry at gunpoint, got nervous, and shot him. Jerry was rushed to the hospital. Six months later the writer saw Jerry and asked how he was doing. His response: "If I were any better, I'd be twins. Wanna see my scars?"

I declined to see his wounds, but did ask him what had gone through his mind as the robbery took place. "As I lay on the floor, I remembered that I had two choices: I could choose to die, or I could choose to live. I chose to live.

"The paramedics were great. They kept telling me I was going to be fine. But when they wheeled me into the emergency room I saw the expression on the faces of the doctors and nurses. I got really scared. In their eyes I read, 'He's a dead man.' I knew I needed to take action.

"Well, there was a big, burly nurse shouting questions at me," said Jerry. "She asked if I was allergic to anything. 'Yes,' I replied. The doctors and nurses stopped working as they waited for my reply. I took a deep breath and yelled, 'Bullets!' Over their laughter, I told them, 'I am choosing to live. Operate on me as if I am alive, not dead.'"

Jerry lived thanks to the skill of his doctors, but also because of his amazing attitude. I learned from him that every day we have the choice to live fully. Attitude, after all, is everything.

What is it about optimism that gives it such power to change not only the way we feel about something but the way it actually is? Just what is optimism anyway? And how can we get a prescription?

The Life Orientation Test[13]

What is your attitude orientation? The following self-assessment by psychologists Michael Scheier and Charles Carver may hold some clues. I have added the second round of scoring to focus your orientation on your work situation.

Round 1: In general, how strongly do you agree or disagree with the following statements as they relate to your attitude? Place a small X in the appropriate boxes.

	A Strongly Agree	B Agree	C Feel Neutral	D Disagree	E Strongly Disagree	Score
1. In uncertain times, I usually expect the best.						
2. If something can go wrong for me, it will.						
3. I'm always optimistic about my future.						
4. I hardly ever expect things to go my way.						
5. I rarely count on good things happening to me.						
6. Overall, I expect more good things to happen to me than bad.						
TOTAL SCORE						

1. Add your scores for 1, 4, and 10 and weight your scores this way: A = 4 points; B = 3; C = 2; D = 1; E = 0.
2. Add your scores for 3, 7, and 9 this way: A = 0 points; B = 1; C = 2; D = 3; E = 4.

What is your total score? If you have a 24, you are unfailingly optimistic. If you have a 0, pessimism rules. If it's a 12, you're neutral. The average score is 14. Two-thirds of people tested fall between 10 and 18.

Round 2: Now, *reflecting on your work situation only,* how strongly do you agree or disagree with the six statements? Place a small "O" in the box that represents your best answer. Compare your X's and O's. Is there a difference? If so, in what way? What can you do to express more optimism at work?

How Optimism Works

WHEN YOU THINK about it, isn't an optimistic attitude slightly dangerous? I mean, isn't there morc of a risk that you will underestimate the potential for danger due to a blithe attitude that all is well? Not really. Pessimistic people are the ones who are fatalistic. They ascribe good and bad things entirely to chance. Because they feel they have so little control, they see no benefit in minimizing risk. Hence, they are more passive, don't think they can effect change, and take fewer preventative precautions.[14]

This fatalistic attitude would be akin to a salesperson listening to a customer's needs, writing a proposal, submitting it to the customer, and then crossing his fingers and letting fate do the rest. The proactive salesperson, on the other hand, will not leave it to chance and will follow up, make modifications as necessary, and not lose touch with the customer.

Pessimists and optimists differ in the way they explain events. According to psychologist Martin E. P. Seligman, pessimists tend to be cursed by the three P's—they are inclined to view events as permanent, pervasive, and personal.[15] Optimists tend to view them as temporary and relevant only to a certain set of circumstances. They assume that they are not the problem.

Permanent

PESSIMISTS TEND TO perceive negative events as permanent while optimists see difficulties as transitory. Pessimists often get so wrapped up in their gloom they can't see a way out. They feel helpless and incapable of changing their situation. Optimists know that "this too shall pass" and help ensure that an obstacle is temporary by making changes.

Clues to the pessimistic outlook in times of adversity are often revealed in the language people use. The pessimist will tend to use extreme, even dramatic phrases like: "I'm ruined," "We'll never recover," and "There's no way out."

Pervasive

PESSIMISTS AND OPTIMISTS differ in the way they view the scope of a problem. Pessimists are absolutists and see problems on a grand scale. They are reprimanded at work by their boss and think they are courting unemployment. Optimists, on the other hand, are experts at damage control. They limit the problem to its borders and refocus on the things that are working well.

As an example, a pessimist might miss a deadline for a report, imagine that her boss is angry, think her boss will view her as incompetent and recommend her dismissal, which will create a money problem, which will cause a missed mortgage payment, which will force the bank to foreclose, which will put her and her family on the street as homeless people.

In the exact same circumstance, the optimist will focus on the quality of the report, apologize for its lateness, and learn what to do differently the next time in order to meet the deadline. No homeless person here.

Personal

"DON'T TAKE IT personally" is a phrase pessimists don't understand. They are their own worst enemies, blaming everything that happens to them or someone else on something they should have done, or didn't do. Self-recrimination dances in their heads all day with thoughts like: "If only I hadn't invited Mary to the meeting she wouldn't have been caught off guard and embarrassed by the CEO's question." Optimists, however, see themselves as personally involved but they don't "own" everything. They deal in the realities of what they have power over and stand aloof from those they do not. They might say, "Too bad Mary muffed the CEO's question. It was a chance for her to shine."

Here's another example: Two department heads in the same company experienced an unusual and disturbing rise in turnover among their employees. James took it personally and blamed the defection on the allure of the dot-com start-ups and his own inadequacy. By not taking responsibility for solving the problem, it persisted. James was immobilized.

Maria was equally disturbed by the turnover and saw it as a call to action. She requested help from the human resources people to stop the leakage. Together they interviewed departed employees. Once the top three reasons for the defections were discovered, she took action to eliminate them. Within two months not only had the hole in the dike been plugged but Maria actually got one of the defectors to return.

In the turnover example above, James took the turnover problem personally and became defensive. Maria didn't even try to place blame. The turnover in her department had to be stopped and she led the charge.

How Optimism Can Turn Around a Tough Work Reality

WITH THE SPATE of downsizings and layoffs that occurred in the 1990s, millions of hardworking employees were put on the street. The tough reality is that overnight they experienced dramatic loss of income and often of self-esteem. An article in the *Detroit Free Press*, "Optimists Are Back at Work Faster after Job Loss,"[16] cites research that indicates that how well people recover from traumatic situations is greatly influenced by "whether they explain their situation to themselves optimistically or pessimistically." In other words, does the jobless individual brood about the dark cloud or does he or she look for the silver lining?

For pessimists, the loss of a job is indeed traumatic and induces self talk like: "This is permanent. Being fired ruined everything. It's all my fault." This negativity keeps them jobless longer since they not only feel but reinforce the feelings of defeat and hopelessness. Faced with the same reality, optimists adopt a different attitude. They see the dislocation as temporary, see the firing as beyond their control, and realize that it's only a job after all and they will be able to get another one.

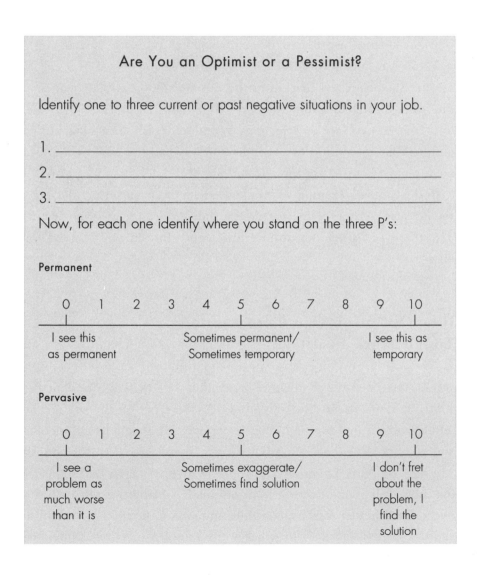

Are You an Optimist or a Pessimist?

Identify one to three current or past negative situations in your job.

1. _____

2. _____

3. _____

Now, for each one identify where you stand on the three P's:

Permanent

```
    0    1    2    3    4    5    6    7    8    9    10
    |                        |                        |
```

| I see this as permanent | Sometimes permanent/ Sometimes temporary | I see this as temporary |

Pervasive

```
    0    1    2    3    4    5    6    7    8    9    10
    |                        |                        |
```

| I see a problem as much worse than it is | Sometimes exaggerate/ Sometimes find solution | I don't fret about the problem, I find the solution |

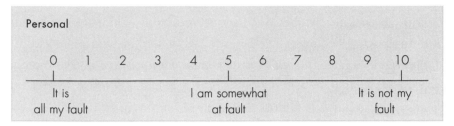

Creating a New Reality for the 3 P's

1. Review the three negative situations you listed in the previous exercise.
2. Now build a case that will allow you to move your ratings to a 10 or close to a 10.
3. How can you interpret each of the 3 P's to lessen their negative impact and use them as a springboard for positive action? Use your imagination.

When you are able to accomplish this, you will have created your own reality. The events are the events, how you interpret them and use them to your benefit are the variables.

The "Hired-Power" of Attitude

SPRINGING FROM VIRTUALLY the same set of circumstances, pessimistic and optimistic attitudes yield dramatically different results. The *Detroit Free Press* states that "optimists tend to be less damaged by the loss of their job. They are back at work sooner. In fact, the attitude of the job applicant often weighs as heavily as the experience listed on the résumé." This is because companies looking for outstanding customer service personnel look for the optimistic attitude first and the skills and experience second. Case in point, Mardi Gardner.

Few people are happier or more upbeat than Mardi; her smile arrives

ten minutes before she does. She had just moved to Miami's South Beach
and was looking through the help wanted ads when she read about a front-
desk position at Ian Schrager's trendy Delano Hotel. Mardi had absolutely
no hotel experience—zilch—but since she had no other interviews
scheduled that day, she figured she'd go just for the fun of it.

Mardi had little expectation of landing the job, and once she saw the
line snake down the street with hundreds of applicants, she was certain
she didn't have a snowball's chance in Miami. Still, she stayed, and after
a few hours of chatting with newfound friends, she had a cursory
interview—a couple of minutes, tops—and left.

When Mardi got the job she couldn't have been more elated, or more
incredulous. She had spent so little time being interviewed she figured
she had been dismissed out of hand as unqualified. Why did they choose
her? The interviewer told her that first impressions are particularly critical for front-desk personnel, who, although they carry out relatively
quick transactional duties with the guests, are usually the first encounter
guests have with the hotel. The image front-desk persons project is the
one most likely remembered.

The Delano tries to replicate that "quick transaction" situation in their
hiring practices for front-desk positions, only spending a few perfunctory
minutes with each interviewee. After all have been seen, in this case
hundreds, they step back and ask: "OK, which applicant comes to mind
quickest?" The first thought was of Mardi's easy smile and vivacious
spirit. The Delano hired her knowing guests would find her attitude
equally impressive and memorable. The rest they figured they could
teach her.

Recruiters of customer-services personnel, such as those at the Delano, know that it is a whole lot easier to improve the knowledge or
skills of an individual than it is to change one's attitude. That's why
they "hire the smile." The preferential treatment given to attitude in the
hiring process is not exclusive to front-line positions, however, as was
made evident to me during a customer-service workshop I gave for employees of a 700-person high-tech company.

I asked the group's members this question: "If you were hiring your internal supplier—that is, the person whose work is directly passed on to you—what characteristics would you look for?" Seventy percent of their responses were directly related to attitude: responses such as "a hard worker," "positive," "team player," "high integrity," "good listener," and "caring about people."

Not only do optimistic people create more enjoyable and memorable experiences for internal and external customers, they also happen to outperform their counterparts. Met Life, for example, increased its share of the personal insurance market by 50 percent once it began using optimism as a hiring criterion.[17] After two years on the job, moderately optimistic insurance agents outsold their pessimistic counterparts by 37 percent, and highly optimistic agents outsold them by 88 percent. Even those who failed to meet Met Life's standard test criteria—but were hired because of their optimism—outsold pessimistic test-passers by 57 percent.[18]

Whom Would You Pick to Replace You?

1. If you were hiring a replacement for your own job, list the top seven attributes or characteristics you would look for in the ideal job candidate.
2. Now place the seven attributes in order of importance with the most important being number one. There are three different characteristics to look for:

   a. Skills (e.g., "An excellent programmer")
   b. Knowledge (e.g., "Understands the tax codes")
   c. Attitude (e.g., "Strong work ethic")

3. Next to each of your seven attributes, place an "S" if it is a skill, a "K" if it's knowledge, and an "A" if it's attitude.
4. Now count the number of S's, K's, and A's. What does this count tell you about attitude?

How to Be an Optimist

OPTIMISM CAN BE a habit like double-checking budget numbers, accomplishing important tasks first, or making tomorrow's to-do list before leaving work. Some of us are natural optimists. Research on twins separated at birth found that much of our disposition to look on the bright side of things is genetic. Current thinking is that perhaps 50 percent of how we view life is predetermined.[19] That leaves 50 percent we can work on. Plus, we can offset our learned helplessness and tendency to focus on the negative by practicing a change in our "mind-style."

How to Think Like an Optimist

OPTIMISM TAKES EFFORT, regardless if it comes naturally to you. None of us is happy when we lose a sale, misspell a word in an important business letter, or blow a presentation. It's hard to stay positive when this world seems built to fall apart, when the forecast for stress is as predictable as the sun coming up, when disappointment and disillusionment are as hard to shake as a bad headache. So how do you overcome those clear and present realities? The happiest people, according to social scientist Alex Michalos, "actually think about being happy and can tell you things they do to be happy."[20] Following are a few ideas to get you thinking and doing.

Use downward comparisons. Psychoanalyst Susan Vaughn suggests using "I'm glad I'm not" rather than "I wish I were" comparisons. Here's an example of how this works to enhance our self-esteem instead of our inadequacies: In the 1998 Winter Olympics figure skater Michelle Kwan said simply, "I didn't lose the gold—I won the silver." Her focus was on what she had accomplished, not on what she hadn't.

At work we can become so focused on what is yet to be achieved—that new account, the promotion, the whizbang industry-shattering development—that we often neglect to take time out to recognize previous accomplishments. This doesn't mean to rest on your laurels. To the contrary, it is intended to enable you to move forward with renewed enthusiasm. The what-have-you-done-for-me-lately school of management disregards this approach under the mistaken belief that people respond better to pressure than recognition.

Put on a happy face. Psychologist William Glasser says, "If you want to change attitudes, start with a change in behavior." Studies have shown that the act of expressing happiness will actually make you happier. Foremost, express your happiness when you're happy with your performance. Make it a habit: when you find yourself preoccupied with tasks—like reading or writing a memo—take a second to acknowledge satisfaction with a smile.

Reward Yourself Right Now

Think of three areas of your job where you can acknowledge yourself for a recent achievement or significant progress toward one that is under way.

1. _____

2. _____

3. _____

---

30 Days to a Better Smile

IT IS SAID that it takes 30 consecutive days of practicing a new habit to replace an old one. For the next 30 days try to reprogram yourself for greater happiness. You can start by doing things like reading the comics, viewing the Comedy channel, renting comedy films, or simply reading those little witticisms and jokes that friends e-mail you.

Use your smile to cheer yourself and those around you. Look for the humor in challenging situations. Smile when you make eye contact with someone. Write the word SMILE in bold letters on a Post-it note and put it on your bathroom mirror where you will see it at the start and end of every day.

Invest in others. When you invest in others, whether by socializing frequently or working on something you believe in—a charitable cause, for example, or an important civic project—you are involved in something big and broad. When this happens your personal concerns naturally seem smaller. Perhaps this is part of the reason extroverts tend to be the happiest people. They alone don't constitute their world. As *Synchronicity* author Joe Jaworski points out, when you invest in an ambition that transcends your self-interest, good things happen and people who can help you achieve that ambition magically appear in your life.

Become a pleasure seeker. Interesting, isn't it, that it is the *pursuit* of happiness that is a right, not happiness itself? The difference? Happiness, as we said earlier, must be a choice. It isn't a destination, it's a process. This is born out in the research that proves the happiest people do *pursue* it. Think about what puts you in a positive frame of mind at work, and pursue it.

Create a Positive Work Environment

SALESPEOPLE ARE KNOWN for instilling their work environment with inspirational triggers to keep themselves thinking positively. One telecommunicator often looks in a mirror when a tough customer is on the other end of the line. At the base of the mirror is the word *Smile*. Another salesperson taped the words *Be Best* to the inside of his attaché case so that whenever he opened it in a customers's office, he would be reminded to be just that.

Take an audit of your office or work space. How does it feel when you enter it? Is there anything that creates a negative feeling for you? If so, get rid of it. What could you change or add to create a more positive or supportive environment? How about photographs of loved ones, awards, inspirational sayings?

Get physical. Nothing can change your attitude faster than a good workout. The effects of exercise on attitude are well documented but not as well heeded. Not only does physical exertion create a biological chain reaction that releases feel-good chemicals into the blood, but a healthy body image also enhances self-esteem, one of the four strongest predictors of happiness.

Confront your fears. When you start imagining the worst, interrupt yourself, and snap out of it, literally if you must. If fear is a nagging habit, some suggest wearing a rubber band around your wrist. As debilitating trains of thought arise, confront them with a snap that sends you a tactical signal to stop stewing over your fears.

Avoid negativity. Judi Sheppard-Missett, CEO and founder of Jazzercise, Inc., says "I believe it is important to surround yourself with people who lift you up."[21] That's because emotions are catching. This can be good, of course, because it helps us share each other's joys and burdens. It is also okay, however, to avoid negative people or situations that can steal your joy for no good reason. Sometimes it's a matter of conscious denial: refusing to read the paper or deciding to turn off the evening news. Sometimes it's a matter of avoiding having lunch with your disgruntled coworker because you know you'll have to work hard the rest of the afternoon not to let his thoughts damage your perspective.

Remember the Benefits of Being in Shape

1. Recall a time when you were in better physical shape. Select five
   words to describe how you felt. Indicate what shape you were in
   by placing an X on the number that best describes it.
2. Circle the number that best describes your current shape.

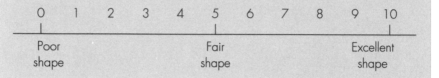

| 0 | 1 | 2 | 3 | 4 | 5 | 6 | 7 | 8 | 9 | 10 |

Poor shape   Fair shape   Excellent shape

3. If there is a negative gap between where you were and
   where you are, what can you do to close the gap?

TRANSFORM ADVERSITY INTO ADVANTAGE

Adversity reveals genius, prosperity conceals it.

— HORACE

IT WAS LATE Friday afternoon and Michael Sullivan was looking forward to the weekend. On his way out the door, he was called into his
manager's office. Bad news. He was laid off. Nothing personal was
meant by it. He was just a "victim" of downsizing. Michael gathered up
his things, said his good-byes, and left the building numb.

This was really bad timing, not just for Michael, but for his company
as well. The last thing the print department where he worked needed
was one less pair of hands. It had been incredibly busy for a couple of
weeks and a looming deadline meant that without him, Michael's former coworkers were never going to make it.

Overcome Your Fear

1. Identify one of your worst fears at work.
2. Write a description of this fear by completing the sentence, "My greatest fear at work is

   _____

   _____."

3. Now imagine every detail of your worst fear described above until it becomes very real to you. Tell yourself what would happen by completing the following: "When this happened

   _____

   _____."

4. Continue pushing the sequence of events to their worst conclusion by adding, "And then what happened was

   _____

   _____."

5. Repeat this until the consequence of your situation is entirely played out.
6. You have projected a challenging scenario. Is it really as bad as you imagined? What could you do to minimize the damage? What can you do to prevent it from happening in the first place?

Fast-forward a couple of days to 8 A.M. Monday morning. Guess who was the first one in to work at the print shop? Michael Sullivan. Why? Because his friends at work desperately needed him and Michael Sullivan wasn't the type of guy to let his friends down, pay or no pay, job or no job. He rolled up his sleeves and went to work. End of story? Hardly. Michael was hired back and promoted through a number of positions and departments. Eventually he went into sales, where he proved to be one of the best salespeople the company ever had.

If you look closely at resilient people like Michael—people who transform bad things into good, people who grow stronger in the face of obstacles—what distinguishes them from those of us who see ourselves as passive prisoners of fate is not the circumstances themselves. They obviously feel they have the power to change their circumstances.

Babies are happiest when they have the power to effect change over their environment, such as the ability to move a toy; the elderly in an assisted-living environment are happiest when they have autonomy over their surroundings; and on the job, people are most satisfied when they have power to affect the work they produce—the power, for example, to shut down an assembly line to correct a defect.

In short, the happiest people are those who act as masters over their fates and not *victims* of it. It is a feeling of powerlessness—real or perceived—that makes people frustrated, angry, and miserable.

Who Lifts You Up?

1. List the ten people you spend the most time with at work.
2. In the space below or on a piece of paper put each name in the appropriate column.

Lifts Me Up	Weighs Me Down

3. How can you spend more time with the "Lift" people and less with the "Weigh" people? Who can you add to the "Lift" column? Who can you eliminate from the "Weigh" column?

NOTE: If the people you listed were to make a list, which column, "Lift" or "Weigh," would they put you in?

The Power of Self-Mastery

AT WORK, WE choose to be either passive and powerless or active and open to self-mastery by learning new skills and uncovering unknown strengths. Jim Anastasi, the owner of the Thunderbird Gift Shop where he sells Native American art and totems, is a perfect example. He loves his work.

He speaks knowledgeably and with great pride about the pieces in his shop, acquired from fifty-eight tribes around the country. Jim says he has found his niche, where he's able to combine his life's passion with his life's profession.

But it wasn't always that way. When his mother was diagnosed with cancer in 1989, he chose to quit his job in the purchasing department of an electronics company to care for her at her home. She passed away a year later. Afterward, Jim was on the street looking for employment in a tight economy. Jobs were scarce and he found no open door.

At his home he was always able to make things grow, so he figured he might as well grow some profit from this talent. He rented a small storefront and began to sell plants. As a display, in his shop window he placed several types of cactus. To give them a sense of their origin in the Southwest, next to them he placed two kachina dolls—which are used as an intermediary between the spirits and our world on this earth—given to him years earlier by Native American friends, who understood his passion for Native American culture.

One day two window shoppers came into Jim's store. Ironically, they weren't interested in the cactus plants, but dearly wanted to purchase the kachina dolls. Because of their sentimental value, Jim refused. Undaunted, they persisted, raising the initial offering price. Equally undaunted, Jim rejected it, stating that they simply meant too much to him. They tried again and Jim flatly stated that they were priceless.

It was obvious to the two would-be buyers that Jim was attached to these objects. As Jim tells it, "It turns out that they were Native Americans themselves. They asked why, if I cared so much about this type of art, didn't I sell it. They offered to supply me with more!" At that moment the Thunderbird Gift Shop was born.

Jim used the adversity in his past to carve out a future. In essence, he turned the tables on adversity and grasped opportunities when others would be paralyzed with powerlessness.

Taking Advantage of Adversity

HOW DO YOU take advantage of adversity? It's a matter of redirecting your feelings of powerlessness into a force for championing your skills and strengths. It's a way to get your voice back, your power back, to get moving again and to use whatever bad happens to you, even the horrible stuff, to fashion a future reality that ultimately both validates and vindicates your suffering.

Find the Gifts

1. Think of the worst disaster you've encountered in your work: a lost job, a demotion, not being hired for your dream job, a performance nosedive.
2. Think of all the ways in which this disaster has been or may become a blessing in disguise. Use your imagination to find the good news or opportunities in the bad news. These opportunities could be big, like starting the career you always really wanted after being fired, or small, like enrolling in a training program to acquire the skill whose absence cost you a promotion.
3. Which of the opportunities on your brainstorm list has not yet been realized? Prioritize the opportunities and set a timeline for the top one on your list. What steps do you need to take to get there by your deadline?

CREATE A POSITIVE LIFE STORY

Reality is what we take to be true. What we take to be true is what we believe. What we believe is based upon our perceptions. What we perceive depends upon what we look for.

—GARY ZUKAV,
The Seat of the Soul

IMMIGRANTS ARRIVING IN New York harbor often view the Statue of Liberty holding her torch aloft as a symbol of relief from adversity. Visitors approaching downtown Enterprise, Alabama, will see a similar-looking statue, smack-dab in the middle of the road in the middle of the town center. As they approach this carved goddess, they may be very surprised at what it is she is holding aloft. It isn't a torch. It's a bug! It's not just one of the ugliest creatures known to man, it's also one of the most destructive: the boll weevil, Enterprise's claim to fame.

The Boll Weevil Monument was dedicated in 1919, two years after Enterprise's Coffee County produced more peanuts than anywhere else in the nation. In 1892 the boll weevil started to invade the South. By 1915 the weevil had invaded cotton crops to the point that handpicking the bug off the plants was tantamount to shoveling in the middle of a snowstorm. Some 60 percent of the cotton crops in the county were devastated, many farmers ruined, and the economy destroyed. But when botanist George Washington Carver came along preaching his revolutionary idea of crop diversification, the citizens of Enterprise eagerly adopted it. Enterprise didn't just survive the infestation, it thrived at peanut production. Ultimately, they erected the monument to remind them of how the town's greatest adversary, the boll weevil, became its greatest triumph.

So what's your monument? What ugly thing can you hold aloft and say, "Isn't it just beautiful?" Like honoring the infamous boll weevil, it comes down to making your personal history work for, not against, you.

Slant Your Life Story

TWO MEN ARE riding an elevator in New York City when a slow smile of recognition comes to one of them. He catches the eye of the other and says: "Joe! You may not remember me but many years ago you fired me from Irving Trust after I'd worked there for seventeen years. I just want to thank you because my life has become so much bigger and brighter since then, and it's all because of you." Joe, looking uncertain, took the man's card. It read "Theodore Borman, President—T. H. Borman Associates, Inc."

Almost twenty years earlier, two men were riding an elevator in New York City and the tension between them was palpable. The raw silence was finally broken as one turned to Ted Borman and asked, "How ya doing?" All Ted could get out was a terse "I'm miserable and I still don't believe you did this to me." The elevator stopped first at Ted's floor where Irving housed its "Hawaiian Suite"—a temporary office where all the "aloha" pariahs from a recent corporate shake-up could work at finding work. As the elevator doors closed and rose without him to the floor where he used to work, Ted's humiliation and wrath combusted. He found his makeshift desk, put his head down, and cried angry and bitter tears.

The most recent elevator encounter would have fared far differently had Ted not been able to create a positive reality around this disaster and others that soon followed. He had reason to be angry and resentful then. He was sucker-punched. Not only had he received no warning of his firing, but up to that point he had been told his work was stellar. But because he viewed his life story in a way that created gifts out of adversity, he thanked Joe sincerely rather than berating him.

The way Ted sees it, getting fired was his first big break. It stirred in him a passion for out-of-work executives, which led to his signing on with a small, family-run executive search firm. Nepotism and politics soon put Ted out on the street yet again.

He then signed on with a larger firm specializing in bio-tech recruiting, which was a natural for someone whose father was a physician. Ted felt as if his eagle had landed and would have happily spent the rest of his career there when his work world fell apart for the third time. His company's bid to go public soured, and the firm's partners, including Ted, were asked to take a 40 percent pay cut. From that moment forward Ted resolved that his destiny would never again be in anyone's hands but his own. Today he is at the pinnacle of his career as the head of his own highly successful bio-tech executive recruiting firm.

Spanning the two elevator rides was a life story that had taken Ted from the depths of despair to the heights of accomplishment and satisfaction. His life story is an internal monument honoring the disaster in his past: a boll weevil of a bumbled, insensitive firing without which he may never have found his true passion.

Creating such a positive life story yourself is a way to express your self-esteem, optimism, and control—three out of the four factors so critical to a happy daily reality. When you add how you've affected and been affected by others along the way, the extrovert part is included as well.

Your ability and willingness to create *your* own reality at work can have a profoundly positive effect on the productivity and joy you experience in your job. When you can *be an optimist*, you embrace the reality of your work life as it unfolds in the present and from there identify and capitalize on those critical elements that will account for immediate success. When you *transform adversity into advantage* you map out future actions that will be the building blocks from which to construct the successful career you seek. And when you *create a positive life story*, you focus on the past as you reinterpret the events that constitute your personal history in such a way as to provide power and nourishment as you move forward.

Create Your "Career Story"

Try this "life-story" exercise I adapted from a similar one by Betty Sue Flowers, a professor of English at the University of Texas.

- **Round 1:** Using only facts from your career as you remember them, create a brief life story that depicts you as a *hero*. Tell your story out loud to yourself or another person. Allow no more than two minutes for this.

- **Round 2:** Using only facts from your career as you remember them, create a brief life story that depicts you as a *victim*. The facts you use may be the same or different from those in your first scenario, but they should be facts as you remember them. Again, present your two-minute scenario out loud to yourself or a partner.

- **Round 3:** Using only facts from your career as you remember them, and which may or may not include those cited in the first two rounds, create a brief life story that depicts you as a *learner*. Present your two-minute scenario out loud to yourself or a partner.

You have now created three convincing, fact-based interpretations of your career. Which is true? Which is the real you? The answer? They are all true and they are all you. So what story have you actually created for yourself? What story are you putting out there in the world when you talk to colleagues, managers, potential employers, and yourself? And here's the big question: Is the story you created supporting you and helping you get what you want in your life? If not, why not create a story that does?

- **Round 4:** Using only facts from *your life* as you remember them, create a positive story for your work life. Convert the negative into positives, the failures into victories. Your reality is yours to create.

Action Steps

BASED ON THE information and exercises in this chapter, complete the following:

- I will start . . .

- I will stop . . .

- I will do more . . .

- I will do less . . .

- I will do differently . . .

F O U R

Get Out of Your Own Way

We have met the enemy and he is us.

— POGO

Y OU IDIOT!" "WHAT a loser!" "You're pathetic!" "If I had you for a partner I wouldn't even show up!" Harsh words, indeed. They were directed by one of my tennis-playing friends at himself. This was hardly what I expected or wanted to hear when I buried my work concerns in my "end of week" to-do list, and headed out the door of my office Friday a liberated man. Jack's self-abuse was annoying, and it was getting in the way of the fun I had anticipated with my Saturday-morning tennis partners.

"Your grandmother could hit that serve harder than you!" "Hit the damn ball, you jerk!" "I GIVE UP!" With this final proclamation of exasperation, Jack let off a roundhouse swing worthy of Mark McGwire and whacked the yellow ball up over the fence into the heavens. He then smashed his racket to the ground as the rest of us simply stood back in amazement. The match was ruined.

Why was Jack so bound and determined to do himself in? To be, as Pogo says, his own enemy?

Self-Sabotage on the Job

SUCH SELF-SABOTAGE IS obvious in all areas of life, but especially in business. Its various forms include the chronic procrastinator, the perpetually late, the people-pleasing promise breaker, and the brilliant underachiever. But why? What is going on when we self-destruct? Is it fear of success? Is it a passive-aggressive way of saying we don't want to do something? Is it fear of risk, failure, or growth? Our self talk holds the clues.

Jack's tirade amplified his internal motivation, the self talk that goes on all the time in our heads. All thinking is a form of self talk, modulating and informing our behavior by past experiences and new information. When we were children we were spoken to, corrected, admired, and admonished, and we internalized these voices, these internal mirrors and road signs telling us who we were and what life was about. Some of those voices helped increase our confidence, discover our abilities, and avoid costly mistakes. Others came in the form of debilitating rules, roles, comparisons, standards of unattainable perfection, or downright meanness. And when these self-defeating voices show up, usually when we need them least, they can act like a perverse traffic cop directing us away from the highway and off the cliff.

Motivation and Self-Sabotage

PAUL WIEAND IS a man who took a mighty tumble, and he has traced the roots of his downfall to his seventh-grade math class. Although he didn't know it at the time, he suffered from a learning disability. In front of the class his math teacher branded him with these humiliating, indelible words: "You're so stupid, Paul. You don't belong here." In high school, Paul graduated in the bottom 5 percent of his class.

Years later, Wieand more than proved his math teacher wrong. "I was determined to prove anyone who ever thought I was stupid, wrong," he says. He graduated from college with a 4.0 in economics; at thirty-three was named president of Independence Bancorp, a multibillion-dollar bank based outside of Philadelphia; and at thirty-seven was a shoo-in as its CEO. While Wieand was celebrating the imminent appointment with his wife in Paris, the board back home was politicking for his resignation. Days after his return, Wieand went from king of the hill to the Dumpster. "Without my position, I didn't know who I was," says Wieand. "I lost my identity." Suddenly he felt as if he was back to being the stupid kid in seventh-grade math. What happened?"[1]

What happened was that Wieand tried to silence with raw power and willpower the pervasive voice that said he wasn't good enough. "Stupid" in math? He became a whiz at finance. "You don't belong here"? He took on the established hierarchy of bankers by trying to force them out, installing younger MBAs to oversee them, and freezing their careers. He swaggered over the board and ultimately committed organizational seppuku when he championed himself as CEO to them, despite the fact that he was less senior than his more influential contender. "If I had listened, I would have heard people warning me to slow down," Wieand says. "But I started thinking that I knew better than everyone else."[2]

Wieand got in his own way because he didn't know that the voice driving him wasn't confidence. It was insecurity. With newfound time to think about what drove him, Wieand returned to school to get his Ph.D. in psychology and now helps other executives rediscover their authentic selves at his Center for Advanced Emotional Intelligence in Bucks County, Pennsylvania.

Trace Your Motivations

LISTENING TO WHAT voices drive you is reality testing. Did you go into finance because you loved math or because some math teacher called you stupid? Do you use your power to effect change or placate your ego? Do you refuse to listen to advice because it is bad advice or because it means someone might know more about something than you do?

We are inventive and clever in the many ways we can torpedo our own boat. Three antidotes I and others have found most helpful are:

1. Discover where you stop yourself.
2. Embrace your mistakes.
3. Claim your genius.

Let's take a look at how our inner voices, when hypercritical or self-limiting, can be the reason behind our self-defeat; how mistakes, which can be our greatest ally in our attempt at excellence, are often shunned and buried; and how the voices of rules, roles, and comparisons can prevent our natural genius from revealing itself and elevating us to the level of happiness and success we've been seeking.

DISCOVER WHERE YOU STOP YOURSELF

JACK, THE FRUSTRATED tennis player, was chastising himself. But let's suppose it was someone else — let's suppose it was you. Imagine that every time you made an error or misplayed a shot, Jack stopped the action and yelled "You idiot!" "What a loser!" "You're pathetic!" "You're plain worthless!" You might not say anything, or you might laugh it off initially, hoping Jack would realize his bad behavior and ease up. You might let Jack know that his comments were wearing thin and he should stop. Likely, Jack's brutal critique would ruin your concentration and performance on the court and destroy any chance of enjoying the match.

"But," you may ask, "didn't John McEnroe win seven Grand Slam titles with such outbursts?" Yes, but *Sports Illustrated*'s Sally Jenkins estimates he could have doubled his Grand Slam wins if he could have handled his unseemly outbursts as well as he handled his opponents' serves.[3]

Tantrums like Jack's don't, of course, just happen during tennis. They happen in all aspects of life, including business. One sees them at work when a sale is lost, a letter mistyped or a deadline missed. They can occur in the executive suite or on the shop floor.

I remember a competent editor who held herself to a "zero-defect" standard. In one document, she uncharacteristically let three obvious mistakes slip through. Sure, it never should have happened, but it did. She was so hard on herself she made Jack look like the benign Mr. Rogers. She was merciless about her failures. For several days her productivity and effectiveness lapsed. Her inner tirades served no positive purpose.

Most of us have a harsh voice like Jack's. The only difference may be that we don't let ours speak in public. But don't be fooled, just because others can't hear doesn't mean it's not there. Often as brutal as a Marine drill sergeant, this ever-vigilant and all-knowing arbiter of good and bad helps us distinguish between what is and isn't acceptable, whether we are interested in hearing it or not. This voice will critique our work products, our work relationships, even our work habits. Nothing is immune. It will tell us how we have performed, "Boy, you really blew that one!" It will even go so far as to tell us how we *will* perform, "I can't believe you volunteered for that project . . . remember the mess you made of it the last time?" In the process it eclipses that naturally gifted performer—the "unconscious competent" within us who has the innate capacity to accomplish great deeds.

When Are You Your Own Worst Critic?

1. List at least five times at work when you have criticized yourself, either aloud or silently, without mercy.
2. What are the common circumstances or patterns in these five incidents? Even if it's not obvious, try to find a similarity. This pattern represents the type of situation when you will be most likely to unleash the self-critical part of yourself.

The Critic at Work

My job is to make sure Elizabeth doesn't screw up. She's an incompetent and if I don't watch her closely she'll make a mess of whatever she is doing. As sure as the sun will come up tomorrow morning she will blow it.

The problem is that ever since she was a young girl she has been slow on the uptake and careless. She just can't seem to follow directions because she has the attention span of a gnat. Sometimes I think she's getting better and then, wham! she reverts to her old self.

Who do you imagine is the author of this minitirade? Elizabeth's boss? Her mate? Parent? None of the above. It is Elizabeth herself. Unconscious as it may be much of the time, it is one of her inner voices, the inner critic, who is passing judgment on her with so heavy a hand and dreary a voice.

Hal Stone and Sidra Stone are two clinical psychologists who originated a powerful self-management process called "voice dialogue." As described in their book *Embracing Your Inner Critic*, everyone utilizes inner voices to help judge their own behavior and performance.

We use this internal dialogue to process information, to pump ourselves up, and, sometimes, to derail ourselves. This sometimes occurs for good reasons such as when we need to distinguish our bad work from our good work. While the inner critic is an example most of us can understand, there are many more. Some of them are described below. See if you recognize yourself in any of these ten voice types:

1. *The Inner Critic*: Pointing out flaws and potential problems is the primary mode of this voice. It will help us to know good from bad and what is appropriate and what is not. On the other hand, it can tend to feel like a nag and in so doing it suppresses positive energy. A good job fit: accountant.

2. *The Controller*: By urging us to recognize and heed appropriate limits and rules, the Controller helps us stay in control when things run

amok at work. On the downside, this voice's need to control can inhibit spontaneity. A good job fit: project manager.

3. *The Wondrous Child*: This delightful little voice is that of the adventurous child who loves to explore and is thrilled with the surprises such journeys offer. Naive adventure, on the other hand, can be dangerous and may lead to getting lost in the organizational woods. A good job fit: researcher.

4. *The Pleaser*: This is the one whose life seems to be dedicated to pleasing people — even strangers. The dominant motive is to be liked or loved. This voice is sensitive to feelings and therefore helps us work well with others. On the other hand, the Pleaser can shy away from tough decisions to avoid hurting feelings. A good job fit: team member.

5. *The Worrier*: Constant fretting seems to be the primary tone of this voice. On the positive side is its ability to recognize obstacles to success. The downside is that the worrier can become frozen by concerns and not take action as needed. A good job fit: planner.

6. *The Wounded Child*: This voice will vary depending on the nature of the wound. For example, Paul Wieand was driven by his learning difficulties. Good job fit: depends on the wound.

7. *Mr./Ms. Responsibility*: This voice demands that people act "maturely." The upside is that it leads to a very responsible, reliable person. The downside is that being ultraresponsible inhibits responsiveness. Good job fit: financial officer.

8. *The Missionary*: The Missionary is out to save us. It takes on the evil in the world and is drawn to the underdog. A noble voice at times, it too can become an additional burden because it takes on others' problems as its own. Good job fit: personnel manager.

9. *The Mind*: This voice is always thinking, trying to figure things out. Often it is a superior analyst whose lessons and conclusions are

helpful. Too much thinking, on the other hand, can dilute or nullify passion. Good job fit: consultant.

10. *The Perfectionist*: The strength of this voice is that it will be the first to find mistakes of any kind. Its burden is that the perfectionist is like Sisyphus pushing the boulder up the mountain. It will never get there because nothing is ever perfect. The strength of this voice is that it will be the first to find mistakes of any kind. Good job fit: editor.

Do any of the voices seem familiar? Note that these only represent the most common voices. You usually have several and there are many others, including Macho Man, the Competitor, the Visionary, the Protector, Aphrodite, and the Little Imp.

When your internal dialogue is working well, it's guiding your decisions and helping you cope with difficulties. The problem is that these voices can almost imperceptibly move from helpful to disruptive. How do you react to someone who always thinks he or she has the right answer, or tries to control you, or is highly critical of you and others around you, or worries so much he or she just sits there, going nowhere as the wheels spin away? At times like these, the voices are unwelcome and inappropriate. When they are in full force they can be a detriment to your effectiveness in business.

Listen to Yourself

TO GET OUT of your own way when one of your voices has shown up, listen to yourself. Use these examples to try to catch yourself in self talk. Identify the inner voice that is guiding you—either in a positive or negative direction.

1. Identify your most dominant inner voice. This will be the one you circled in the following exercise.

2. Identify examples of how this voice supports you at work. For example, maybe your "Pleaser" helps you understand and have empathy for the needs of the people who report to you, allowing you to keep them motivated.

3. Now identify examples of how this same dominant voice undermines you at work. For example, the very same Pleaser might be reluctant to confront two team members who are at odds so as not to hurt their feelings.

What's Your Dominant Inner Voice?

Place a check next to the inner voice(s) that you recognize in yourself, and identify how you incorporate this role into your current job. In the empty spaces add any of your voices that are not on the list. Circle the voice that is most dominant.

Voice	Job Role
1. Inner Critic	_____
2. Controller	_____
3. Wondrous Child	_____
4. Pleaser	_____
5. Worrier	_____
6. Wounded Child	_____
7. Mr./Ms. Responsibility	_____
8. Missionary	_____
9. Mind	_____
10. Perfectionist	_____
11. _____	_____
12. _____	_____
13. _____	_____

Manage the Voice

Stick to three concepts. You can't help everyone. You can't change everything. Not everyone is going to love you.

ROBERTA VASKO KRAUS,
sports psychologist

THE FIRST STEP in managing one of your voices is to notice when it shows up. This means being able to monitor your self talk and not just react to it unconsciously. The second step is to identify and acknowledge the message you are trying to send to yourself. Whether you agree with it or not, by simply acknowledging the voice you will be able to reduce its persistence and volume. The third step is to harvest what is worth keeping and use it to increase your awareness and skills at the office.

Charles had just finished a formal presentation to a buying committee of five people. All in all, the presentation went well, but was not perfect. Andrea, Charles's manager, had attended it, and in the car on the way back to the office she noticed that Charles was upset. "What's up?" she asked. "Boy, did I blow it," said Charles. "I ran over the time limit, didn't allow enough time for questions, fumbled the CFO's price objection, and even misspelled a word on the flip chart. And there's more. I wasn't—"

"Whoa!" said Andrea. Charles's inner critic had gone on a rampage.

"If you could change three things, what would they be?" she asked. Instantaneously, Charles was able to slow down his spiraling negative judgments. After hearing the three "do-overs" from Charles, and acknowledging them as useful for further development, Andrea asked, "And what did you do well?" With his inner critic at rest, Charles was able to appreciate the many aspects of the presentation that went well. In the end, the inner critic, managed effectively, had done its job and so had Charles and Andrea.

Though your first reaction may be to silence your inner dialogue especially when it's negative, when you come right down to it these voices will never be silenced, nor should they. The frequency of their appearance can be moderated, their stridency can be lessened and when they do show up they can be *managed*. Learn to use them. Once you develop an awareness of your inner dialogue, you will be able to be an objective observer and decision maker in your own work life.

Getting out of your own way is a matter of recognizing and managing your inner voices, and never are those voices more important than when they tell you that you've made a mistake.

EMBRACE YOUR MISTAKES

I sometimes react to mistakes as if I have betrayed myself. My fear thus seems to arise from the assumption that I am potentially perfect and that if I can just be very careful I will not fall from heaven. But a mistake is a declaration of the way I am now, a joke to the expectations I have unconsciously set, a reminder I am not dealing with the facts. When I have listened to my mistakes I am wrong.

—HUGH PRATHER,
Notes to Myself

REMEMBER MY TENNIS partner Jack? It was his mistakes that were irritating him to the point of making himself and others around him so miserable. But who ever heard of anyone playing a perfect game of tennis? Even world-class competitors battling it out in the finals at Wimbledon will make a good number of mistakes—euphemistically known as "unforced errors." So why do we expect nothing but perfection on the job? The simple fact of the matter is that the only way to avoid mistakes is not to try. And perhaps that is the biggest mistake of all.

At work, no matter how hard you try, no matter how careful you are, no matter how much you want to be perfect, sooner or later you will make a mistake. The question is not whether we make mistakes, but how many we make and how we deal with them when we do. The simple truth of the matter is that in any job, too many mistakes will mean unreliable performance, and unreliable performance eventually translates into an unreliable performer. At this point, low performance ratings are earned and your job security will be at risk. Just as with Wimbledon, the winner in business is usually the one with the most winners and least "unforced errors."

Not All Mistakes Are Created Equal

THE IMPORTANT THING is to deal with mistakes so that you both minimize their impact and maximize what you learn from them. Once you adopt this point of view, you will have created a strong defense against the marauding inner critic. And not all mistakes are created equal. For example, an error that results in the loss of a customer is much more serious than showing up late for a staff meeting. But, as regrettable as these serious miscues are, they do occur. The drama and severity of the consequences they cause can have a profound impact on the person or persons who made the mistake. But even with such powerful consequences, the mistake itself, whether large or small, is always a form of performance feedback.

When a mistake occurs you can wallow in self-criticism or you can use it for future improvement. If upset and remorse is appropriate, then be upset and remorseful. But to stay in that place and not mine the error for future lessons is a second mistake on top of the first. In a way, it's a wasted mistake.

128 Richard C. Whiteley

Mistakes Become Teachers

THE AVIATION BUSINESS is a place where people take mistakes seriously and learn from every one of them. As Steven Meyer, a private pilot, began to descend into Los Angeles's John Wayne Airport he realized that the landing gear on his recently purchased private plane would not engage. The tower told him to continue trying to get his wheels down, circle in a holding pattern, and wait until his fuel was spent. A couple of frantic hours later, the plane belly-landed and was smothered in foam to prevent an explosion. Meyer lost the plane but he walked away unscathed. Enter the Federal Aviation Administration (FAA).

The FAA, which takes extraordinary pains to reconstruct accidents and determine their root causes, spent months investigating the causes of the mishap. They found the cause of the malfunction was a faulty bolt, but the point was not to apply blame but to gain knowledge to be used to inform, educate, and ultimately prevent a repeat accident.

Similarly, if we are to succeed at work, it is critical to understand the reasons behind our errors and how to prevent them from happening again. So one of the kindest things you can do for yourself is to "go to school" on your mistakes.

Given that most of us sincerely want to do our job well and truly want to be counted among the top performers at work, let's take a look at three different types of mistakes.

The first kind, *Derailer* mistakes, makes us miserable because they enter our lives for no apparent reason and throw us off the track. The second kind, *Inner Saboteur* mistakes, occurs when we create the errors unconsciously and unwittingly sabotage ourselves. They often signal discomfort or unhappiness and ultimately represent an escape from an unpleasant situation.

Finally, there are the *Go-for-It* mistakes. These occur when we are pushing the envelope, and because we are in new territory, we stumble. That stumbling is an indication of our willingness to take risks in search of a greater purpose or end.

How Do You React to Your Mistakes?

1. Identify at least three mistakes you've made on the job in the last year. Include both small and large mistakes.
2. How did you respond? Think about your emotional response, how you discussed the mistake with others, and what you did to fix it.
3. Thinking about the specific situations you identified, circle the number below that best describes where you typically are in the balance between beating yourself up for a mistake or learning from it.

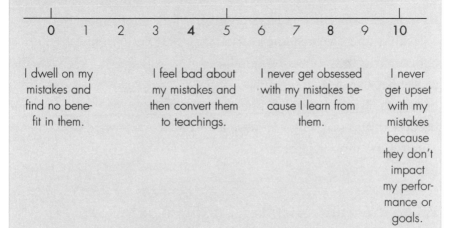

| 0 | 1 | 2 | 3 | **4** | 5 | 6 | 7 | **8** | 9 | 10 |

I dwell on my mistakes and find no benefit in them.

I feel bad about my mistakes and then convert them to teachings.

I never get obsessed with my mistakes because I learn from them.

I never get upset with my mistakes because they don't impact my performance or goals.

4. If you are out of balance and berating yourself for your mistakes rather than learning from them, what can you do to shift the balance to learning?

Derailer Mistakes

DERAILER MISTAKES CAN kill momentum, kill enthusiasm, and ultimately kill career opportunities. If you are struggling with your job and want to locate and correct the cause of these performance inhibitors, consider a performance self-analysis.

Inner-Saboteur Mistakes

SOMETIMES WE UNCONSCIOUSLY create mistakes because we really don't want to succeed. While this hidden motive for creating errors is rare, it occurs enough in business to examine it here. Often it shows up as the low performer who is fired, takes another job in another company, and flourishes.

For example, Barbara never seemed to be able to generate the kind of sales numbers that would secure her a place in her company's high-performer category. In spite of working for one of the best managers in the company and being in a territory with high potential, she couldn't seem to get it together and was eventually fired. Undaunted, she signed on with a direct competitor and today, selling in the same territory as before, she is the number two producer in its entire sales force. Whether it was her manager, the company culture, the products, or something in herself, Barbara couldn't find the groove at the first company, and because of this may very well have fallen into a downward performance spiral of her own creation.

What Are Your Mistakes Telling You?

Performance Self-Analysis

To discover where you are stopping yourself, answer these questions:

1. Do you know what is expected of you?
   - If No, this may be the cause of your making mistakes. Make sure you are clear about what is expected. Discuss expectations for your work with your manager. Review your job description and performance objectives.
   - If Yes, this does not appear to be a problem. Go to the next question.

2. Do you have the skills to do what is expected of you?
   - If No, this may be the cause of your making mistakes. List the skills that are critical to your success and rate your proficiency in each. (3 = Very Strong, 2 = Some Strength, and 1 = Needs Development.) Have your manager do the same and compare notes. What programs, reading, or developmental experiences can help you improve the 1's?
   - If Yes, this does not appear to be a problem. Go to the next question.
3. Do you have the resources required to do what is expected of you (e.g., time, budget, staff, tools, management support)?
   - If No, this may be the cause of your making mistakes. Identify what specific resources you are lacking. How can you acquire what you need? If appropriate get your manager to help requisition the appropriate support.
   - If Yes, this does not appear to be a problem. Go to the next question.
4. If questions 1–3 are answered Yes, are you performing with minimal or no mistakes?
   - If No, you may have a motivational problem where the work is boring or not worth it to you. Consider reengineering your job, as described in chapter 1, "Follow Your Passion."
   - If Yes, keep up the good work!

IF YOU ARE mistake prone at work and can't understand why, you may be in a situation similar to Barbara's. To check, do the following:

1. First, answer the four questions in the Performance Self-Analysis above.
2. If your response is Yes to all of them, ask yourself if this is really the job or project for you.

3. Make a list of the things you don't like about your specific situation and study them. In particular, look at the resources available to you. Are there external factors that are making it difficult for you to perform well? What are they?

4. What can you do to eliminate or minimize the external factors that are holding you back?

If you find yourself in such an intolerable circumstance, don't assume there is no way to change your current assignment. Talk to your manager or someone in human resources and determine what options are available to you. The key here is to find a fit between a talented and willing you and the job that has to be done.

I have often seen this misalignment between a person's nature and his or her work in sales. The job of selling really requires two quite different types of people. The "hunter" is the person who is great at creating customers from nothing. He or she can start in new, undeveloped territory, make the calls, and close the business. The "farmer," on the other hand, hates cold calling and prospecting but is a genius at working with existing customers to find solutions for them that continually yield a growing stream of orders. While some salespeople embody both the "hunter" and the "farmer," they are very rare. The job-matching problem occurs when you put the "farmer" or the "hunter" in incompatible situations. Inevitably both will struggle and, most likely, fail.

Are You Afraid of Success?

The following quiz is a *Fortune* magazine adaptation of a questionnaire developed at Boston College and published in *The Success-Fearing Personality* by Donnah Canavan, Katherine Garner, and Peter Gumpert.[4] I have modified it further to focus on your situation at work. While it isn't foolproof, it should give you a pretty good idea of where you stand. If these statements apply to you, answer yes. Then figure your score as described below:

1. I generally feel guilty about my own happiness on my job if a colleague tells me (s)he's depressed at work.
2. I frequently find myself not telling others about my fortune at work so they won't have to feel envious.
3. I have trouble saying no to people at work.
4. Before getting down to work on a project, I suddenly find a whole bunch of other things to take care of first.
5. I tend to believe that people who look out for themselves first at work are selfish.
6. When someone I know well succeeds at work, I usually feel that I've lost out in comparison.
7. At work I rarely have trouble concentrating on something for a long period of time.
8. When I have to ask others for their help at work, I feel that I'm being bothersome.
9. I often compromise in situations to avoid conflict at work.
10. When I've made a decision at work I usually stick to it.
11. I feel self-conscious when someone who "counts" at work compliments me.
12. When I'm involved in a competitive activity (sports, a game, work), I'm often so concerned with how well I'm doing that I don't enjoy the activity as much as I could.
13. A sure-fire way to end up disappointed at work is to want something too much.
14. At work, instead of wanting to celebrate, I feel let down after completing an important task or project.
15. Mostly, I find that I measure up to the work standards that I set for myself.
16. When things seem to be going really well for me at work, I get uneasy that I'll do something to ruin it.

SCORING: Give yourself one point for every question you answered Yes to, except numbers 7, 10, and 15. For each of those, subtract one point if you answered Yes. Anything under 5 points means you're basically OK. Between 5 and 10 points, you're moderately at risk for self-sabotaging behavior. Between 10 and 16 points, you have a problem.

Go-for-It Mistakes

THE THIRD TYPE of situation occurs when you really want to succeed and the mistakes help you. They are the "Go-for-It" mistakes.

Business author Tom Peters understands the power of failure when he advises us to become a "failure fanatic." He says, "The more failure, the more success—period."[5] Accomplished entrepreneurs know this better than anybody. Show me a successful entrepreneur and I will show you a failure. It is the rare business creator who hasn't tried and failed, sometimes numerous times, before hitting the jackpot. Thomas Edison went to the drawing board ten thousand times before he was successful in creating the incandescent lightbulb. Abraham Lincoln lost nine attempts at public office, but won three, one of which was the presidency. We, of course, could go on and on with more examples of successful failures because there are few great people alive today or in history who have not suffered great defeat.

When a panel of three highly regarded and successful entrepreneurs was asked how they felt about failure, an amazing thing happened. No one seemed to understand the question! The word *failure* simply doesn't exist in their business lexicon. Sharon Whiteley, winner of *Inc.* magazine's "Entrepreneur of the Year" award said, "Failure is only the opportunity to try again with more perfect information!" For these people it is not all or nothing. They understand that on the road to success making mistakes is part of the journey—unpleasant, even disappointing at times, but nonetheless inevitable.

High-Performance Mistakes

RICK WAS THE Midwest regional manager of a software company. Although his company's primary clients were in the financial services industry, when the Ford Motor Company requested a proposal for a huge contract, the temptation was too great. Despite the fact that the conservative automotive industry highly values automotive industry experience in its vendors, Rick proceeded undaunted. Many considered his decision to be foolhardy.

In a monumental effort, Rick and his team produced a comprehensive proposal. The associated time and expense was enormous and the opportunity cost of not pursuing other more natural new business opportunities was great. The competitive bake-off, as it was called, started with twelve potential suppliers and was gradually whittled down to two. Amazingly, Rick and his team were one of them. But when the final decision was made, they weren't selected. The Ford buyer cited "industry experience" as the deciding factor.

With the news of the loss it wasn't long before the spoken and unspoken I-told-you-so's were evoked. Rick's "fool's errand" had cost the Midwest region mightily and had jeopardized its ability to make the year's revenue targets. The only remaining question was would such a mistake in judgment cost Rick his job. Hardly. Although one might say he used poor judgment, his boss, the president of North American Operations, appreciated that it was a go-for-it mistake. He realized that Rick's willingness to go "where angels fear to tread" had potential payoff if they could break into the highly lucrative automotive market. Rick's "mistake" had helped gain valuable knowledge and experience, and even an enhanced reputation for the innovative approach he and his team took in responding to Ford's request. Accordingly, the president awarded a discretionary bonus to Rick and his team. His vision and confidence were rewarded two years later when 40 percent of the Midwest region's revenues came from the automotive industry.

Bruce Fernie, founder and chairman of Tealux, Inc., a chain of tea bars, has the same philosophy as Rick's boss. He looks for people who have experienced adversity when he hires executives. For him, their setbacks represent precious lessons. He says, "If they have nothing but successes, that scares the heck out of me. I want someone who's seen it all, who's ridden the rocket up and down. Because you learn a lot more coming down."[6]

The quality movement of the late 1980s and early 1990s brought us the concept of using mistakes to continuously improve performance. In Japan, this is called *kaizen* — making continuous improvements in small increments as stepping-stones to perfection. *Kaizen* encouraged workers to bring their mistakes to light so that they could be corrected, saving time and money as well as helping to create a better product. In fact, in many Japanese factories a series of buttons have been installed on a production line so that any worker who caught something faulty could stop the line. Previously only shift supervisors were authorized to take such preemptive actions. Incredibly, when a worker did execute this privilege, other workers on the line would stop and cheer. That was one mistake that would never find its way to a customer.

Embracing the concept of high-performance mistakes means that you open yourself up to their inevitability, learn from them, and correct them to help yourself and others in the future.

Using Your Mistakes

> *You will never have it all together. That is like trying to eat once and for all.*
>
> —ANONYMOUS

NO ONE GOES through a single day, yet alone a life, without making his or her share of mistakes. When you do, rather than let your inner critic have a field day, you have the opportunity to show yourself some compassion. At such a time anthropologist Angeles Arrien asks, "Is my self-worth as strong as my self-critic?"

If you are making too many mistakes, consider completing the "Performance Self-Analysis" on page 130 to help you reduce or eliminate them. And, following that, when they do happen, follow these steps:

1. Express your disappointment. Get through whatever tantrum or upset needs to express itself.

2. Forgive yourself for the error. Forgiving yourself means acknowledging what happened and then *letting it go*. Not doing this keeps your attention and energy in the past and sets you up for more mistakes in the present.

3. Clean up the mess. Whatever damage your error caused, do what you can to set it right.

4. Learn from it. Take responsibility for knowing what caused the mistake. Use the Performance Self-Analysis to identify root causes and come up with a plan about how to prevent the mistake in the future.

5. Mine the mistake. Are there any new insights or unexpected applications that can come out of your mistake?

Richard Bach nicely sums up this philosophy in his book *The Bridge across Forever*. He says: "That's what learning is after all. Not whether we lose the game but how we lose and how we've changed because of it. And what we take away from it that we never had to apply to other games. Losing in a curious way is winning."

CLAIM YOUR GENIUS

Each of us has not only a "genetic code" but also a
"genius code."

— BARBARA MARX HUBBARD,
former Democratic
vice presidential nominee

CIRCLE YOUR ANSWER to this question: Are you a genius?

YES   NO

When I ask audiences this question, less than 1 percent will raise their hands to signify a YES. Out of one recent group of 500, for example, only three had the courage or belief to put their hands in the air.

Those other 497 people were wrong and if you circled NO above, you may be too. The dictionary defines *genius* as "natural ability," "exceptional or transcendent intellectual and creative power," or "a natural talent or inclination." Notice the word *natural*. It's the gift you were born with, that extraordinary something that makes you unique. Most of us think of genius in a MENSA intelligence-quotient kind of way. Intelligence at that lofty level, is only one form of genius, only one test of talent.

When I have asked audience members who raised their hands why they did so, they usually confide that they have a genius IQ. In other words their intelligence has been externally validated and with this kind of sanction they are able to claim their own genius, even in public. My invitation to you is to unmask your authentic, natural genius by stripping away the encrusted layers of what you think you are supposed to be instead of who you are.

Psychologist Brian Schwartz says, "People will only achieve the level of success that their image of themselves can absorb."[7] So how is it that we lose contact with our "self" and pull the plug on our own natural genius? I can think of several reasons: The first is rules, the second is roles, and the third is comparisons.

Rules

I TEACH A workshop to businesspeople called, "Rediscovering the Artist Within: Sketching for People Who Can't Sketch." As you might guess, the goal of the workshop is to help people find the creative part of themselves that they may have buried and then take it back to their jobs. Last year I was working with Harold Montgomery, founder and CEO of Checktronic, a successful Dallas-based company serving the financial industry. Harold came to me for a one-on-one session in hopes of reconnecting with his childhood ability to draw. Like most people, he was constricted by the rules that had been imposed on him in his journey to adulthood.

Imagine walking into a class of twenty first-graders and having the teacher announce that you are going to teach them how to draw. If you ask the class, "How many of you are artists?" every little hand will shoot into the air. Now try the same thing with twenty of your business colleagues. My guess is that at best only a couple of hands would be raised. What happened to that enthusiastic little creator? Why do we shut down when it comes to being creative in our own work situation?

First, Harold drew a wineglass as he normally would. With a little anxiety he produced a scratchy and constricted reproduction of something that remotely resembled the goblet in front of him. The lines on the sketch pad reflected his tension and he immediately rejected it, stating it didn't look anything like the real thing.

He then drew the wineglass again, this time following the three rules that are the key to liberating the creative artist within. They are:

1. **Focus**. Only look at the object you are drawing. Do not look at the sketch pad.
2. **Contact**. Keep the pen on the pad at all times. It must remain in direct contact with the paper. If you take the pen off, the drawing is done.
3. **Flow**. Keep your hand moving until you are finished. If you stop, you are thinking about the drawing, and this exercise is about *not thinking*. It is about free-flowing creativity, so if you pause, even for a moment, the drawing is done.

Once he was released from the "rule" of having to draw a wineglass that looked like one, Harold started to create, to have fun, and to express his natural drawing ability. Then we relaxed the "new rules" and let his objective, rational thinking inform and focus his creativity and passion. Harold was delighted to recapture what had been long lost. He took his revitalized creativity back to his work and released it there. Several months later I got a letter from him with a stunning sketch of a hibiscus, his favorite flower, enclosed.

Identify the Rules

Because of societal rules limiting creativity, anthropologist Margaret Mead believed that 90 percent of our capacity is untapped. Take a moment and consider: What are the rules—long-standing ones or your current company's policies—that limit your natural abilities?

1. _____
2. _____
3. _____
4. _____
5. _____

How would you break these rules?

What Rules Stop You?

WHAT ARE THE rules that inhibit the expression of your genius? Common ones that were imprinted years ago by teachers, parents, and other "big" people are:

- "Children should be seen and not heard."
- "Be brave, don't cry."
- "Who do you think you are?"
- "Don't get too big for your britches!"
- "Grow up!"
- "That's a boy's game."

Creativity-suppressing admonitions continue in the workplace with statements like these:

- "When I want your opinion I'll ask for it!"
- "Who authorized you to do that?"
- "We're paying you to follow the rules, not break them!"
- "Step aside, I'll handle this."
- "It's okay to take a risk, but it better work!"

Roles

Few things cause more fear of success than a sense that if you follow your dreams, you will betray the people who love you.

—ANNE B. FISHER[8]

ROLES ARE MASKS. As with rules, these roles can be internalized at a very young age or can be created by others' expectations of us in a work situation.

In business, quite appropriately our roles are defined by the functions we perform. You may be a whiz at marketing but would absolutely die on the vine if you were transferred to the accounting department. This specialization by training and personal inclination is useful and necessary. On the other hand, sometimes we get slotted into informal roles that confine our natural abilities.

John migrated to such a role. He is a gregarious, happy-go-lucky sort who is always fun to be with. He has a sharp wit, a well-developed sense of humor, and a seemingly endless repertoire of the latest jokes. Being pleasant and amusing at work is one thing, but overdoing the revelry nearly cost John his job.

Because of his upbeat and witty nature, without being conscious of it, John became the comic relief for his work group. When things got tough and people were feeling tense and pressured, they could always count on John to lighten up the group with his humorous antics. Without formal consent, both John and his colleagues agreed that he would take on the role of corporate Good Humor Man.

While this may seem to make sense, it actually turned out to be a burden and career disadvantage to John, because as the company performance pressure rose, so did his pressure to outdo his previous antics. But the "act" became stale and people began to discount the business acumen and sound thinking that really existed behind his mirthful veneer. At first they thought of John as the class clown and later as simply a buffoon. Fortunately, John's manager noticed his slipping credibility and counseled him to stop his role as comedian.

The happy ending to the story is that today John is still his happy-go-lucky self—after all, this is his nature. But released from the implicit responsibility to lighten up the group, he emerged as a respected and vital member of the team.

There are many informal roles people play in business, including the Class Clown, the Disciplinarian, the Judge, the Realist, the Pessimist, the Optimist, the Bleeding Heart, the Tough Guy or Gal, the Know-It-All, the Confessor, the Peacemaker, and others.

What Are Your Roles?

ANSWER THE FOLLOWING to find out.

1. Identify your explicit and implicit roles at work.
2. What expectations do your colleagues have of you because of these roles? Focus on those outside your functional expertise.
3. What expectations does your manager have of you because of these roles?
4. Do these roles support your natural abilities, goals, or personal expectations? If so, how?

If your answer to Question 4 is No, what can you do to lessen or abandon these formal and informal roles in your job?

Comparisons

The greatest artist was once a beginner.

—THE FARMER'S DIGEST

ONE OF THE most powerful and common habits that inhibits our natural abilities is making comparisons. Comparisons can be useful. They offer standards by which we judge good work from marginal effort and they enable us to set a meaningful target for our own personal and organizational growth. Indeed, in recent years, benchmarking—the practice of formally analyzing your business processes relative to industry-leading organizations—has become one of the top tools used by executives around the world. At a personal level, this "going to school on the winners" is exactly what we're doing when we hire an executive coach or consultant. When we approach these comparisons with the attitude of a learner, we can grow and flourish. But there is a dark side to comparisons that occurs when, either consciously or unconsciously, we actually use them to immobilize or demoralize ourselves.

Sometimes what keeps us from acting powerfully is our belief that we are not as smart, skilled, adept, agile, lucky, or experienced as somebody else. Whenever you use the words "not as" it may be a tip-off that you are about to begin a comparison that may stop rather than start you.

- I'm **not as** good with numbers **as** . . .
- I'm **not as** experienced **as** . . .
- I'm **not as** creative **as** . . .
- I'm **not as** well-known **as** . . .
- I'm **not as** skilled with people **as** . . .

At this time what you can do is acknowledge that you are comparing and ask yourself, "So what does this mean for me? Does it mean that the person I'm comparing myself with might do a certain task better?" If you've held the person up as worthy of comparison, then probably he or she would. "Does that mean if I do try I will not be able to create a worthy result?" Probably not. You have a choice. Either don't act— because you believe you will look inferior to someone who has more experience, knowledge, training, skills, contacts, or other resources than you—or take a shot—perform your best, learn, set your sights on innovation, and explore your natural ability in this untried area.

Theodore Roosevelt expressed this idea beautifully in a speech delivered to the University of Paris, Sorbonne, on April 23, 1910:

The credit belongs to the man who is actually in the arena, whose face is marred by dust and sweat and blood; who strives valiantly; who errs and comes short again and again, who knows the great enthusiasms, the great devotions, and spends himself in a worthy cause; who at best, knows the triumph of high achievement; and who, at the worst, if he fails, at least fails while daring greatly, so that his place shall never be with those cold and timid souls who know neither victory nor defeat.[9]

Your Comparisons

THE FIRST STEP in coping with the negative effects of limiting comparisons is to be aware when you are making them.

1. Identify a person at work you compare yourself to and you believe is superior to you. This could even be a person you feel competitive with.
2. What experience, knowledge, training, skills, contacts, or other resource does this person possess that you have not developed or tried?
3. To what extent does it bother you that this person seems to be better than you?
4. If it bothers you that this person seems to be better than you, you are most likely wasting your energy by either not valuing yourself, not valuing the true merits of the other person, or just wishing things were different. Whether you are bothered or not, continue to the next question.
5. Which of the resources you listed in question 2 do you believe are unexploited strengths of yours or can be developed?
6. What can you do to develop these resources?

By taking a developmental attitude rather than a competitive attitude, you will be able to avoid the misery comparisons can cause and channel your energy into productive pursuits.

Make Yourself the Standard

We are all in this together, alone.

— LILY TOMLIN

THE FIRST STEP in getting out of your own way when comparisons loom is to dare to act. The second is to shift the comparison from others to yourself.

Phillip Rubin first contacted me in the early 1990s shortly after my first book, *The Customer-Driven Company*, was published. Phil, a customer service representative at a hotel, has cerebral palsy and dyslexia. He was determined to excel with his customers in spite of his learning and physical issues.

Although I have never met Phil face-to-face, over the past eight years, I have had the pleasure of becoming a mentor to him. Judging from the pile of customer letters praising his efforts it is clear he could be my mentor as well. When Phil compares himself to many of his contemporaries — doctors, lawyers, and successful businesspeople — he gets discouraged. When he gauges his performance against his personal resources, he appreciates himself.

Because there can only be one "best" and because there is only one winner, if we choose to compare ourselves with paragons, by definition most of us are going to be "losers." So if you have to compare and compete, why not make your own personal best the standard? How can you accomplish this? First, appreciate yourself for having stepped into the arena in the first place. Second, assess your performance relative to your potential, not somebody else's achievement. Rather than asking, "Did I do my best?" ask "Did I do my best, given the resources that were available to me at the time?" In this question, "resources" means your own physical and emotional conditioning as well as assets that are external to yourself like time, materials, and supervisor support.

Comparing Yourself to You

1. Return to the untried or underdeveloped resources you identified in question 5 in the previous exercise on page 145. List them.
2. What other natural abilities do you possess? Add them to your list.
3. Assuming you were hiring someone with the attributes you listed in questions 1 and 2, what projects or jobs would you have them undertake in your company? Are these projects and jobs to which you aspire? If so, what do you need to do to make them a part of your job?

Take Stock, Give Credit

> *There is no best in a group of individuals.*
>
> —TAO TE CHING

THE LATIN ROOT of the word *genius* means "guardian spirit"—the natural and magnificent "you" who is your genius. It is yours to claim, nurture, and bring forth in your life to support your own success. As sure as you have a genetic code you do have a genius code. Find and celebrate yours.

Where Is Your Genius?

TO FIND OUT, reflect again on your natural abilities and consider the following:

1. List those abilities that are clear strengths that you are using today in your job. Are there other ways you would like to utilize them at your company or in your career?

2. List your undeveloped, untried, or buried attributes, your unexploited strengths. How could you bring them out in your current
   job? Your company?
3. How would you like to utilize them during the course of your
   career?

Circle your answer to this question: Are you a genius at your work?

YES   NO

I hope you can answer the above question with an unequivocal Yes!
If you're not there yet, perhaps you might ask the question this way:
"Who am I not to be?" Marianne Williamson puts it that way when she
says:

> Our deepest fear is not that we are inadequate. Our deepest fear is that
> we are powerful beyond measure. It is light, not our darkness, that most
> frightens us. We ask ourselves, "Who am I to be brilliant, gorgeous, tal-
> ented, and fabulous?"
>
> Actually who are you not to be? You are a child of God. Your playing
> small doesn't serve the world. There is nothing enlightened about shrink-
> ing so that other people won't feel insecure around you.
>
> We were born to make manifest the glory of God within us. It is not
> just in some of us. It is in everyone. And as we let our own light shine,
> we unconsciously give other people permission to do the same. As we are
> liberated from our own fear, our presence automatically liberates others.[10]

It is ironic but true that one of the biggest obstacles that prevents us
from achieving our goals and fulfilling our dreams at work is ourselves.
In thousands of subtle and unconscious ways we create barriers that
make doing our work more like navigating an obstacle course than
smoothly walking the path of opportunity and fulfillment. With thoughtful introspection and candid self-appraisal you can *discover where you
stop yourself, embrace your mistakes, and claim your genius.* And when

you do, those barriers will come down and your work life will be greatly the better for it.

Action Steps

BASED ON THE information and exercises in this chapter what actions will you begin to take to get out of your own way?

- I will start . . .

- I will stop . . .

- I will do more . . .

- I will do less . . .

- I will do differently . . .

Foster Your Interdependence

*We are all angels with only one wing. We can only fly
while embracing each other.*

—LUCIANO DE CRESCENZO[1]

W HAT A TIME we live in. What fun we are having. It's the wild
west of an entirely new frontier of unpredictable advances that have, in
many ways, made the world a smaller, faster, cheaper, safer, and better
place to live. All of this, however, has not come without a price in
human terms.

Sure, we are more "connected" with satellites, the Internet, and cable,
but are we more in touch? How much of our day is now spent transfixed
on the face of some machine—the TV, the computer, the PDA, the
Game Boy—instead of another person? We are not just plugged in and
turned on; we are positively hot-wired to these machines and more and
more out of touch with one another. As Linda Stone, vice president of
Corporate and Industry Initiatives at Microsoft, puts it, "Technology has
made it easier to contact people instantly but also has made it harder
to get close to them."

Work Is Human

TECHNOLOGY ENHANCES OUR work lives every day—speeding up communication, easing the analysis of large amounts of information, and presenting our ideas in quick, elegant, and spell-checked formats. The problem occurs when we let technology eclipse the human aspects of our existence, when high tech dominates and high touch slips into the background. Although companies like Communispace use technology to build communities across distances and work schedules, it more often pushes people apart instead of bringing them closer together.

This high tech versus high touch imbalance was first highlighted in 1982 by John Naisbitt in his book, *Megatrends*. At that time, it constituted the book's smallest chapter. Now it's the central subject in his latest effort, *High Tech, High Touch*. One of the six symptoms Naisbitt found through his new research on our "technologically intoxicated" society is that "we live our lives distanced and distracted." But technology itself isn't the only culprit.

The Impact of High Tech

"I CAN GO days without seeing a soul, and I'm a professional communicator," says Max McCormick. McCormick went free agent a few years back when his video production department at a large utility was outsourced. Adds McCormick:

> The technological advances in video production and post-production are stunning, exciting, and cheap. Now it is possible for independent producers to produce in-house much of what they used to farm out to others. That's the upside. The downside to all this incredibly good and dirt-cheap technology is that independents tend to become isolated. Personally, with e-mails, faxes, and Web-based research, I have gone days without speaking to another human about my work, even on the phone. Isolation is just a by-product of this new world of work.

High Tech and Your Job

To what extent has technology reduced your personal phone or face-to-face contact with others over the past five years? Check one:

☐	No Change: I have as much personal contact as I have always had.
☐	Modest Change: I have experienced a little lessening of personal contact.
☐	Major Change: I rarely have personal contact with people I used to spend time with, either by phone or face-to-face.

1. How has your job been affected by your answer?
2. To what extent do you see this as a positive or negative change? Or both?

With the need to be streamlined and nimble in a highly competitive global economy, businesses have had to decentralize into smaller, disparate, self-contained units. The traditional vertical hierarchy is dying — and quickly. This flattening and streamlining of the organization — with its virtual offices, remote mobile workers, demise of lifetime employment, and free-agent workforce — has put physical and emotional distance between many of us. Ironically, all of this isolation is occurring at a time when research indicates a tight correlation between the ability to collaborate and organizational success.

Back to the Future: *A Return to High Touch*

BUSINESS WEEK STATES that 78 percent of Americans feel the need for more spirituality in their lives.[2] Not coincidentally, this is up from

20 percent five years ago, a time span that parallels the geometric rise in technology. Why the correlation? In "A Study of Spirituality in the Workplace" for the *Sloan Management Review*, authors Ian Mitroff and Elizabeth Denton write: "If a single word best captures the meaning of spirituality and the vital role it plays in people's lives, that word is interconnectedness."[3] By putting these two pieces of information together we can conclude that most of us are open to, if not seeking, greater interconnectedness or interdependence.

Clearly, it would seem, the further our separation becomes, the greater the corresponding need to find ways to be close. This has also become a critical success factor for companies that seek success in today's fast-paced and rapidly changing business environment.

In businesses today there are fewer managers and supervisors to provide coaching and guidance. Reduced staff and higher-performance expectations have moved relationships in companies from caring and thoughtful to cursory and transactional. Given these circumstances, it is you who will have to take on the responsibility of establishing a network of people who will coach you, applaud you, and blaze a trail for you, making you more effective when you need colleagues to support your ideas and better poised to take advantage of your next career opportunity. To foster your interdependence:

1. Get connected at work.
2. Identify your ideal personal board of directors.
3. Assemble your board.

GET CONNECTED AT WORK

Do you have a best friend at work?

—MARCUS BUCKINGHAM AND CURT COFFMAN,
First, Break All the Rules

JOAN MCCOY WAS shocked not once but twice after she was passed over for a promotion. Everyone agreed that as director of community relations for ARCO Alaska, McCoy was a stellar corporate diplomat. She had proven her first-rate people skills while dealing with several highly sensitive issues with the public. Her first shock came when she heard the news that another person was picked. The second was when she walked into her manager's office to find out what else she could possibly do to get promoted. The answer: Get leadership skills. She couldn't believe that she was not viewed as an effective leader. So she turned to business coach and author Lois P. Frankel.

Frankel conferred with Joan's coworkers and discovered that she was great at handling people—outside the company. Inside the company, however, Joan had isolated herself from coworkers. She didn't delegate. She didn't hobnob. She was courteous but chilly. She rarely asked for anyone's opinion, figured small talk was a waste of precious time, didn't listen well, provided little feedback, and, in summary, found little use for personal interaction with executives or anyone else for that matter.

Not only did she not know how to build a team, her lack of connectedness meant that her achievements were not formally recognized, and few of her peers were even aware of them.

Says Joan, "I thought I would be rewarded if I kept my nose to the grindstone. I never worried about my relationships with coworkers. So I was oblivious to problems that were all around me. Lois told me to invite people into my office. The first person I asked in was incredulous: 'You want me to come in?' That really drove home how isolated I had become. Now I talk to people in the elevator or in the cafeteria. For the first time, I'm getting a lot of good information about what's going on in our company."[4] As evidenced by Joan's experience, getting connected at work may be just as critical to your career path as the actual work you do.

Ways to Get Connected at Work[5]

TO GET INTERCONNECTED at work, Lois Frankel offers these suggestions:

1. Once a day, drop into someone's office for a ten-minute talk. "Casual conversation helps build friendly relationships that can withstand stress."
2. When people talk to you, listen. "Put everything else on hold for a moment, so that people will realize that what they're saying matters to you."
3. When you need help, ask for it. "This is mainly a relationship-building exercise, but you'll get lots of useful feedback as well."
4. Begin conversations with small talk. "If you always talk about work, people will think that you only care about work—and that you don't care about them."
5. Do favors for others, even when you can't anticipate that a favor will be returned. "Doing so builds good corporate karma, and somehow, some way, you'll benefit from that karma."

Interconnect for Superior Performance

RESEARCH DONE BY the Forum Corporation was designed to discover the leadership practices that have the most leverage in creating superior levels of work group performance. One of the surprising findings was that "soft" people-connecting practices like "knowing the capabilities and motivations of individuals in the work group" and "demonstrating care for members of the work group" had the highest statistical correlation with high performance. More traditional "hard" practices like "communicating clearly the results expected" and "communicating the strategy of the organization as a whole" were also important but did not score as high. While both "hard" and "soft" are required for success, it is the emergence of the more people-oriented, connecting practices that are noteworthy.

Mapping Your Network

IN ORDER TO assess how well connected you are at work complete the following:

1. Put a small circle in the center of a blank piece of paper and write the word *ME* inside.
2. From the *ME* circle, draw lines like spokes on a wheel to other circles on the paper, with each new circle representing a person in your company who is important to your success. Put the person's initials in each new circle.
3. Review this relationship map and make sure you haven't left anyone out. Is there someone you could add to enhance your chance of success? If so, add another spoke and circle.
4. Now, next to each circle place a number that reflects the quality of your working relationship with this person: 5 = outstanding, 3 = so-so, and 1 = challenging.
5. What can you do to improve any relationship that is a 1 or a 3? Start with the people who are most critical to your success who have a 1 or 3. What is the nature of the problem? What can you do to fix it? Your future success may be greatly enhanced by your ability to do this.

The correlation between job satisfaction and advancement to hands-on support is nothing new. It wasn't so long ago that, in many companies, the old-boy school of mentors handpicked their most promising prodigies and groomed them to move up the career ladder. With the advent of temporary project-based work versus long-term position-based work, these traditional hierarchies are gone. Today, you are CEO of you, and like all CEOs, much of your success depends on the quality of the support system you have created at work.

Recognizing the importance of providing such guidance to workers has spurred many companies to initiate various forms of mentoring programs. Some are formal, with people actually assigned specific senior leaders to be their guides. Others, more informal, allow ad hoc matching to take place between mentor and mentee. Organizations would do well to pay more attention to this opportunity. Most are not doing it well and it does have a direct bearing on both increasing productivity and reducing turnover. A 1999 study conducted by Interim Services and Louis Harris and Associates indicates that 35 percent of those employees who don't receive regular mentoring have short-term intentions to find another organization that will provide it for them.[6]

If there is no effective system for finding a mentor in your organization, don't wait around for one to show up. Perhaps it is time to recruit one. Even better, you may want to think about bringing together a number of them to compose your own Personal Board of Directors (PBD).

IDENTIFY YOUR IDEAL PERSONAL BOARD OF DIRECTORS

None of us is as smart as all of us.

—POGO

ORGANIZATIONALLY, THE IDEA of having some kind of outside advisory group of experts is hardly new. Corporations have a board of directors. Such a group is usually composed of both company executives and external members not directly affiliated with the organization. This latter group brings with it prestige, connections, and valuable expertise. In the same manner, universities, educational institutions, and charitable organizations have boards of trustees with individuals from many different disciplines as members. In fact, executive cabinets composed of government leaders perform the same function: to help make decisions, set directions, establish positions, and create policy.

Just as group-think works for a company and even countries, the same concept will work for a going concern of one: you.

Your "A" List: One Idea

IN CREATING YOUR own Personal Board of Directors, understand that diversity is vital. A PBD composed of a cross-section of personality types and skills is more powerful than a homogeneous grouping of knowledge, talents, experience, and outlook. What works best is assembling people with different skills, different perspectives, and different personalities. This partnering of differences creates healthy, creative tension as well as powerfully complementary, though unique, approaches.

Identify Your Current Board of Directors

WHETHER YOU REALIZE it or not, you already have a personal board of directors. Although you may not think of them that way, you have already given certain people power to have influence over your work life. Take a moment now and begin to think of who these people are. Write their names down. To help you identify the members on your board, try answering the following questions, and as you do, understand that you may not have a specific individual to fit in every category:

1. Whether they give it to you specifically or not, of the people you know, whose opinion do you respect greatly?
2. Of the people in question 1, from which ones do you actively seek counsel?
3. Of the people in question 2, what kind of counsel do you seek? (job strategy, skills development, problem solving, emotional support, wisdom, etc.)
4. Who provides you with enthusiastic recognition of your work and achievements?
5. Whom do you go to when you have a problem?
6. Whom do you talk to when you have a career or life-planning issue?
7. Who is your current and most powerful teacher?
8. Who is your greatest critic?
9. Who influences you despite his or her toxicity?

You have now listed your current board. After thinking more about your ideal board you can compare what you want with what you have, and see if any changes are in order.

There are many different types or archetypes you may wish to consider for your Personal Board of Directors. Let me describe six of the most common. As I do you may want to consider whether this would be a good member for your board and, if so, who might be a good candidate for membership. They are the Politician, the Strategist, the Problem Solver, the Coach, the Butt Kicker, and the Cheerleader. The exact composition of each individual's PBD will vary. In fact, you may want to add one or two different kinds of archetypes who are not on the list just mentioned, or add new members and release others as your personal circumstances shift.

Let's look at how each of these board-member archetypes works and consider ways of addressing those particular problems you're likely to bring to each one.

The Politician

*If you don't have political skills, your promotion prospects
will suffer.*

—JANE CLARKE,
Office Politics

TODAY IT IS not uncommon for the same employee to have two or
even three different bosses. Or, even worse, all too many find themselves
wondering exactly who their supervisors actually are.

Mary Beth Schoening, the founder of WorkVision, a consulting firm
dedicated to improving the well-being of people at work, sees this con-
fusion among her clients every day. She calls it "work frenzy." Schoening believes that because traditional supervisory relationships have been
so dramatically altered, having a mentor has become a paramount ele-
ment of career success in many companies.

A mentor—someone you can trust as possessing "been there, done
that" knowledge—is the cornerstone of most PBDs. I call him or her
the Politician because the Politician surpasses classic mentoring. He or
she will have two additional characteristics beyond being a role model
and advisor.

First, he or she must know the *political* ins and outs of your organization and be able to offer advice in that context. Every organization
has subtle and not so subtle ways of getting things done behind the
scenes. The Politician knows them. He or she knows what moves to
make, with whom, and when.

Second, the Politician not only knows what maneuvers work, but he
or she is *tapped into the power centers* of your company. This is important because when it is time for this person to take a stand on your
behalf, his or her voice needs to carry weight in the organization. The
mentor who has political savvy but lacks power can be helpful advising
you but won't have a knockout punch to make things happen. Con-

versely, someone with power but little political savvy may be viewed as a loose cannon.

Therefore, an excellent choice for the Politician on your PBD will not only be someone with an aptitude and willingness to sponsor and nurture your aspirations but a person with the political astuteness and power to help bring them to fruition. In most cases, the Politician will be someone who is senior to you.

He or she doesn't have to be an officer or executive but should have some influence with the organizational units along your most likely career path. In many cases this person might be your immediate supervisor — but doesn't have to be. The individual may also be from outside the company. For example, one of Forum's board members, Carol Goldberg, former chief operations officer of the supermarket chain Stop 'N Shop and a member of the boards of Gillette, Selfcare, America Service Group, and other companies, has made it her business to develop a supporting/advisory relationship with several senior managers. She meets with them periodically to advise, counsel, and lend moral support. She also has the insider power and clout to help them make things happen.

When to Call Your Politician

THE BEST WAY to work with the Politician is to establish a formal career review and progress-check every six months. This is best handled during nonwork hours, such as at lunch or dinner. Also meet with the Politician if an unexpected event occurs. For example, if you are asked to take a position in another part of your organization, you may want to contact the Politician for advice and counsel.

The Strategist

> *To have his path made clear for him is the aspiration of*
> *every human being in our beclouded and tempestuous*
> *existence.*
>
> —JOSEPH CONRAD,
> *The Mirror of the Sea*

NEED A CAREER road map? Then get a Strategist. The Strategist will help you devise successful tactics for getting from point A to point B. These tactics may include such issues as how to get additional budget allocated to your key project, how to break down barriers between your department and another group you must rely on for success, and how to manage your workload to bring more work-life balance into your personal situation.

For years my personal Strategist was John Humphrey, a cofounder of the Forum Corporation and a person I worked under for many years. John's strength was the ability to help me clarify what I really wanted, identify alternative paths for getting it, and decide on the approach with the greatest chance of success. I usually went to John with business issues like determining the appropriate deployment of people in the group I was managing, positioning a product in the marketplace, or discovering the best approach for dealing with a particular competitive situation.

The effective Strategist will most likely start any session by determining what it is that you are seeking. Remember, this person's strength is helping you find the best and most direct path from A to B. A is where you are now. B is the destination. Where do you want to go? Often the most beneficial impact a Strategist has is to help you become completely clear about what you want. Once that is done, the appropriate road to get you there often becomes surprisingly obvious.

Strategy Stoppers

List one major career goal below followed by all the external barriers (not having proper equipment, not having enough time) and internal barriers (reluctance to ask for help, procrastination)—as well as their solutions—you can possibly dream up. Don't reveal your solutions with your Strategist. Rather, allow him or her to come up with unprejudiced ideas on his or her own. By comparing approaches you will learn more about strategic thinking.

Career Goal: _____

Internal Obstacle: _____

  My Solution: _____

  Strategist's Solution: _____

External Obstacles: _____

  My Solution: _____

  Strategist's Solution: _____

Getting from Point A to Point B: *When to Call Your Strategist*

ACCORDING TO AUTHOR Ben Stein, "The indispensable first step in getting the things you want out of life is this: decide what you want." Your work in chapter 1, "Follow Your Passion," should help you figure out what that is. Once you know it, it is time to call in your Strategist. Common issues the Strategist can help you tackle are:

- How can I move from manager of my department to manager of the division?
- What is the best strategy for achieving my current year's business objective?
- Given a dramatic change in circumstances (downsizing, introducing a new line of products, a merger), what is my best approach for continued success?

For each path, the Strategist helps you explore all the pros and cons, the potential obstacles, and methods for overcoming them. The key is to identify all the barriers you can ahead of time and work with your Strategist to devise a plan to eliminate or bypass them before they actually occur.

The Help You'll Require: A Strategist's Strength

ANOTHER FACTOR IN creating a winning strategy falls under the category of "help required." In his classic research on high-achieving individuals, psychologist and Harvard professor David McClelland noted that a key to success is clear and strategic use of help. Rather than going it alone, the achievement-oriented person identifies the gaps and soft spots in his or her plan, and seeks the assistance of those who have the knowledge, skills, and willingness to help bolster these weak areas. The Strategist can help you plot out how to play to your strengths by filling in with others who have the strengths you lack.

Prepare for meeting with your Strategist by listing what you believe to be your strengths and areas for development. As before, don't bias your Strategist with preconceptions, but allow him or her to formulate opinions as to what they might be. Later, after you've discussed the Strategist's take on your strengths and developmental areas and compared them with your own, identify what you do well that you can exploit and what's holding you back that needs work.

The Problem Solver

IF THE STRATEGIST uses a telescope to peer into the future, the Problem Solver uses a microscope to look at the here and now. He or she is skilled at helping you examine in detail the day-to-day problems that can stop you cold. First, the Problem Solver will most likely start by having you clearly define the problem. The better the description, the easier the solution. Too often people, upset by something that has gone awry or that keeps them from their goal, have great difficulty in explaining what is actually wrong. This may yield only a generalized fretting and negative downward spiral that inhibits the clear thinking required to define the problem, never mind solving it.

A problem-solving technique called Force Field Analysis can be helpful in sizing up an issue, identifying the factors influencing it, determining what steps will impact the situation, and, finally, settling on the actions that will have the most leverage in making the problem disappear. Developed in the 1930s by the founder of modern social psychology Kurt Lewin, this simple and effective approach helps you identify all the factors affecting your current problem. Here's how Force Field Analysis works:

By literally drawing the dynamics that create a problem, you can see more clearly the circumstances that will alleviate it as in the figure below. For example, imagine your problem is: *My manufacturing team is having trouble meeting new product introduction schedules.*

Problem: *Trouble Meeting New Product Deadlines*

Alleviating Forces		*Creating Forces*
Process improvement teams	◄——►	Inadequate manufacturing process
Training for new employees	◄——►	Inexperienced members of my team
Allowed "flex" time in schedule for unanticipated changes	◄——►	Mid-project revisions from engineering
Some new equipment	◄——►	Old equipment
Motivated and hardworking staff	◄——►	No budget for overtime

When pressure from the *Creating Forces* and *Alleviating Forces* is equal, there is a static tension surrounding the problem. To create an imbalance so that the problem is lessened or goes away:

1. Weaken or eliminate a *Creating Force*.
2. Strengthen or add an *Alleviating Force*.
3. Create a combination of #1 and #2.

In this example, if you can get engineering to reduce the revisions requested, you weaken that *Creating Force* and the problem will begin to go away. Alternatively, if you can get permission to add some temporary staff to work until you're back on track you will add an *Alleviating Force*.

Give the Force Field Analysis a try for yourself.

• Think of a problem you are having at work.
• State the problem clearly and then set up a Force Field chart like the one below by brainstorming every conceivable *Alleviating* and *Creating Force*.
• Now, by adding, deleting, strengthening or weakening the forces, make your problem go away.

Problem: *"My problem is* _____ *"*

Alleviating Forces   *Creating Forces*

_____ ◄──► _____
_____ ◄──► _____
_____ ◄──► _____
_____ ◄──► _____
_____ ◄──► _____
_____ ◄──► _____
_____ ◄──► _____

Working with your own personal problem solver and using such problem-solving techniques will help you identify and eliminate conflicting forces more readily than if you choose to wing it alone.

The Coach

The conductor doesn't make a sound. The power of the conductor is derived from making other people feel powerful.

—BEN ZANDER,
conductor, Boston Philharmonic

ONE OF THE strongest trends in management and leadership development today is the extensive use of executive coaching. Overnight, the art of providing individual counseling to executives has appeared and proliferated. Several years ago the title "executive coach" was rarely known or used. Now, there are literally thousands of these advisors working with leaders and managers at all levels in organizations. There are even a number of Web-based systems that offer online coaching.

Perhaps the popularity of executive coaches has been prompted by today's emphasis on the "learning organization" described in Peter Senge's classic business bestseller, *The Fifth Discipline*. This is a place where not knowing is okay but not trying to learn isn't. It is a place where the human asset is recognized as the only major asset—other than money—that can appreciate. The idea is that in order to create and maintain competitive superiority and outperform rivals, each person in an organization needs to be continuously developed.

How does this relate to you? It relates to you because you are, in effect, your own organization wrapped up in one person. The crucial question is "Are you a learning organization?" Answering yes requires that you say to yourself first—and later to others—"I don't know how to do that," or "I don't know how to do that as well as I would like to." Enter the Coach.

The Politician, the Strategist, and the Problem Solver all help you develop a winning approach to your job and identify and eliminate the obstacles that block you. The Coach, however, is a kind of on-the-job personal trainer, but instead of fitness, he or she can help you acquire new business skills and/or knowledge. If you have repeated areas of underperformance or are heading into new territory, perhaps it is time to add the Coach to your Personal Board of Directors.

In the last few years the process of benchmarking has become one of the methods most frequently used by business leaders to improve their success in implementing new or improving existing business processes. Benchmarking works this way: identify what you wish to start doing or improve, find the company that is the best in the world at doing this particular process, ask them to teach you its methods, become a student, adapt what you learn for your circumstances, and put it into practice.

In speeches, I often ask people to raise their hands if they have ever taken lessons from a professional to help them learn golf or tennis, or if they have hired a teacher to help them learn how to play a particular musical instrument. Many hands go up because at some point most adults have engaged in this form of personal benchmarking. They find an expert at something they wish to achieve and who will teach them how to do it. That's a coach. Yet when I ask audiences if they have consciously created coaches in their work lives, few hands go up.

How to Find a Coach

THE PERSON WHO has developed the skill(s) you wish to bolster could be your coach. It doesn't matter whether this person is above you, a peer, or below you in the organization. The only thing that does matter is whether he or she has the skills you wish to emulate and is willing to help you. Of course, in any organization the first place to look for skills development is in training and other formal developmental programs. Your manager or the appropriate person in your human resources or training department will be able to guide you.

Ideally, your manager has been prominent in collaborating with you to identify the specific areas in which you need to develop—even coaching you in some of them. In smaller organizations, this is less likely to happen. If there is no human resources group, it can still be a beneficial experience to approach your manager and initiate a developmental discussion. The objective: to determine your top opportunities for improvement.

Working with a Coach

ONCE YOU DETERMINE that there are specific skill areas you would like to improve, you can borrow a page from the benchmarking practices of world-class companies in the following five steps.

1. **Identify the areas you wish to develop.**
   - What problems keep recurring?
   - What new activities are you undertaking that will require new skills or expertise?
2. **Identify who has mastered what you wish to achieve.**
   - Inside or outside your company, who has mastered what you want to learn?
   - Which of these people will be willing to help you?
3. **Clarify what you want.**
   - What, specifically, are you asking for?
   - How will you know when you have received it?
4. **Get your prospective coach's commitment to help you.**
   - After specifically requesting what you need ask "Would you be willing to help me?"
   - Also ask: "What way of our working together is best for you given the demands of your own situation?"
5. **Recognize and thank your coach for developing you.**
   - Remember to thank your coach for helping you and perhaps include a small gift or token of appreciation.
   - Ask your coach how you might be able to return the favor.

The key here is to take stock and honestly assess where you have terrific skills and where you need to develop. Be willing to admit to yourself and relevant others what you don't know. This is a big stumbling block for many people. Somehow many of us put pressure on ourselves to be "perfect." This is a curse because it means believing that your ignorance is impossible. If it is impossible, your personal learning organization of one—you—is doomed to the inefficient, grueling, and sometimes painful process of trial and error.

The next step, actually asking for help, is also avoided by many people. Usually those you ask are flattered that you have chosen them as an icon and will be happy to help within the constraints of their normal workload. Because the Coach is usually helping you with a specific skill or knowledge area, it need not be a long-term assignment for him or her.

The Butt Kicker

IN THE LATE 1980s I had been thinking and talking about writing a book on service and quality. I hadn't grown up with the idea of being an author, but a two-week study mission to Japan—where I visited and learned from nine award-winning companies like Toyota, Komatsu, and the Palace Hotel—awakened the writer in me. Awakened or not, the writer inside me hid in the closet and wasn't about to step out and actually do something. Too risky. Too hard. Too busy.

After a lot of talk, Pat McLagan, a successful author, professional colleague, and friend who for some time had been gently encouraging me to write that book, uttered these fateful words: "Enough, Richard, stop talking and start writing!"

These words hit me like a drill sergeant's command. We all know people like Pat who are not only familiar with our aspirations and talents but will not rest until we are at full potential on both. These are the Butt Kickers.

Corporate board members are expected to challenge a company's leadership to stretch the organization to its full potential. My experience is that there are usually one or two Butt Kickers on every board who are going to challenge the status quo and continually probe for unexploited assets and opportunities. These are generally good-spirited folks who aggressively endorse mottos like the U.S. Army's "Be All That You Can Be."

Dream the Big Dream: *When to Call Your Butt Kicker*

WHAT WOULD YOU do at work if you knew you couldn't fail? List one to three things you would take on. Who can you share your aspirations with who will keep you accountable (read "kick your butt") if you don't go for it?

The Butt Kicker is the one who won't let you settle for a too comfortable job, career, or life. This is the person who will demand that you reach your potential and, if necessary, change significantly to do so. Just as Pat McLagan did for me, this person will challenge, goad, and push you to move out of your comfort zone.

The Butt Kicker and Challenge

WHEN A BUTT Kicker challenges you, it may even make you angry because you know—deep down inside—that he or she is right. You don't want to be pushed out of that comfort zone you have created for yourself. You may even feel a little guilty for resisting.

The key to selecting this board member is to pick someone you respect and, equally important, someone who respects you. A parent or spouse probably wouldn't be the best person for this role. Why? Because the Butt Kicker's motivation in this case might be more rooted in his or her own personal aspirations for you rather than your own. You need someone who is solely focused on you.

Marcia Wieder, author of *Making Your Dreams Come True*, declares that as long as you're dreaming you might as well dream big. What is it that you want in your job and career? Don't be shy about getting clear on this and then sharing it with a Butt Kicker you can trust. Of course, just because you can articulate your dream doesn't mean it's going to happen, but your big dream has a much better chance of being realized if it is stated explicitly to yourself and backed up with someone who won't let you give up on it.

The Cheerleader

> *The deepest principle of human nature is the craving to* *be appreciated.*
>
> —WILLIAM JAMES

TOO MANY ORGANIZATIONS are run on the belief that mature people can make their way in life without someone patting them on the back all the time. This all-too-common attitude flies in the face of what we know about the human condition. Whether we admit it or not, it is the rare individual who, at some level, doesn't appreciate a sincere compliment. Mark Twain wrote: "I can live for a month or two on a good compliment." Whether it's for two months or ten minutes, the Cheerleader's role is to appreciate you and give you the affirming compliments you need.

In a classic work on organizational climate, George Litwin and Robert Stringer studied organizations with high-performing work environments and those that performed at lower levels of effectiveness. From this research they developed a questionnaire to measure the key variables that make up the superior work climate. One factor they measured is summarized in the statement, "In this organization compliments outweigh criticism." Not surprisingly, they discovered that high performance work climates are created when "compliments outweigh criticism."[7]

In some toxic business environments, unfortunately, criticisms far outweigh compliments. The problem is that people often see no sense in commenting favorably on that which you are supposed to do in the first place.

Conversely, researcher and author Don Tosti finds that compliments serve an important function at work: "motivational feedback." Compliments make employees feel like a valued part of the work team. On the other hand, Tosti categorizes criticism as "developmental feedback." Appropriate criticism serves a valuable purpose — to drive professional development — and has greater impact when it is paired with compliments. Tosti believes that the ideal time to offer motivational feedback is immediately following a performance event. Conversely, he believes the time for developmental feedback is later, after the emotion and adrenaline of the event has subsided.[8]

For example, Jane had just finished making the first of several presentations to people in her company about the proper use of the new voice messaging system. Adrian, her supervisor, attended the first session and noticed some things Jane did well and others on which she could improve. After a small group of questioners dispersed, Adrian approached and asked Jane if it was a good time to fine-tune the presentation, indicating that she was going to point out what went well and hold suggestions for improvement until a later time. Adrian proceeded to point out all the things that Jane did well: her organization, the quality of the PowerPoint material, how she answered questions directly and clearly, her natural enthusiasm, and how she handled a sensitive issue raised by the senior vice president of her department. While this was going on, Jane felt like a strong, competent, and worthy performer. (Adrian may have even asked Jane if there were other things she felt she did particularly well and compliment her on those.) At the end of this first segment of feedback, Jane felt appreciated, clear on what things went well, and motivated to repeat them in future sessions.

Adrian shared developmental feedback just before Jane's next presentation. Jane was geared emotionally for the seminar and focused on how she could improve on her first effort. What might have sounded like redundant and harsh criticism immediately after the first session now felt like advice.

The Negative Power of Criticism

TO UNDERSTAND THE effect of negative criticism, try this brief exercise.

1. Find a friend to work with (let's call him Paul).
2. Ask Paul to extend one arm to the side and parallel to the floor. *Check to make sure he has no shoulder or arm problems.*
3. Ask Paul to resist as you place your hand over his wrist and begin to put gradual and gentle downward pressure on it. Gradually increase the pressure until his arm begins to go down and then release your hand.
4. Now ask Paul to think of something about himself that he doesn't like and to nod and resist when he has it. When he nods, start exerting downward pressure on his wrist with the same intensity as before. You will both be surprised that his arm is much weaker and requires much less pressure from you to move down.
5. Now ask Paul to think of something he loves about himself, nod, and resist. As you increase your downward pressure at his wrist you will both be amazed at how much stronger he has become. You will have to exert much more pressure to even budge the arm. If you ask Paul to think negative and positive thoughts about another person, the same result will occur.
6. What can you learn from this exercise?

Negative criticism can be toxic. Eight years ago, I was teaching a critical "pilot" seminar to a group of engineers from a large high-tech manufacturing company. At every break, no matter how long or short, my client contact—the person responsible for setting up the program—

would rush up from the back of the room and, with thinly veiled panic in his voice, tell me everything I was doing wrong. The program was actually going quite well, but I had a nitpicker on my hands.

The criticisms were distracting and forcing me to shift my attention from the executives — my real audience — to him. In effect he was undermining his own pilot. Finally, during a break, I assertively asked him to comment only on what was going well unless he saw something that truly threatened the success of the pilot. Once he shifted from criticism to compliment, I was back in focus and the program was successful.

Some people are more comfortable waiting for the developmental feedback while others feel a sense of tension as they wait for the other shoe to drop. The key is to try out different approaches to see what works best for them. As you think about your Cheerleader, remember he or she is not there to tell you what you did wrong, but to tell you what you are doing right.

Create Your Own Cheerleader

IN ADDITION TO the Cheerleader, there is another little trick that can help keep you in a positive frame when things go awry. It is a "Yea File" — an actual manila file folder with that title. Whenever you get a verbal or written compliment, note it and put a copy in your Yea File. Letters, e-mails, and notes go in there, as well as complimentary voice-mails that have either been typed or simply jotted down. At times when you need positive reinforcement, bring out the Yea File and start reading. When people do this, without fail, they are always uplifted.

ASSEMBLE YOUR BOARD

THE FIRST STEP in assembling your Personal Board of Directors is to list the types of members you believe will benefit you most. Consider the Politician, the Strategist, the Problem Solver, the Coach, the Butt Kicker, and the Cheerleader. You may want to substitute for or augment these types with others. For example, consultant Christie Jacobs has the Connector on her board. This is a person who seems to know everything about acquiring the best equipment, services, and deals available. Whether it is a new printer, baby-sitters, health food, or which of the dizzying array of telephone services to use, you can bet the Connector has researched the options, has the best solutions, and will be only too happy to share them with you. Far from hoarding this priceless and time-saving information, the Connector loves when other people "go to school" on them.

A good way to identify who might be a helpful board member is to ask this question: Where am I unsure or struggling in my work life? List the most critical areas where you need support. You have just created potential board "seats." After you have listed the specifications for your Personal Board of Directors, it is time to start filling the positions. The first step in doing this is to consider who is currently on your board.

As pointed out at the beginning of this chapter, if you are like most people, you have surrounded yourself with people who have considerable influence over what you do and don't do, the decisions you make, and how you feel about yourself, others, and the world in general. Because you allow these people to have such influence, they are currently on your board. You may also have paid board members, such as tax consultants, lawyers, financial advisors, and fitness trainers.

If you have put your personal advisory group together consciously and explicitly—and by explicitly I mean you have formally asked these people to support and help you—then you are well on your way. Not surprisingly, however, most people have not been this systematic in arranging their support. Yet at the same time they do have "natural" influencers, people in their lives who have an impact on them—whether formally requested or not. For example, a manager in a high-tech firm said that with all the turmoil and change in his company in recent years he has chosen to follow *his manager*. His reasoning: "He is a person I trust and respect, so wherever he goes I will do just fine if I follow." In this case, whether there was an explicit agreement between the two or not, this person has at least a board of one and his manager is akin to the Politician.

Your Ideal Personal Board of Directors

LOOK AT YOUR original list of ideal board types. Note the members of your current personal board of directors who are fulfilling these roles, whether you have asked them to or not. As you review your current and ideal PBD, consider:

- Who do I want to add?
- Who do I want to excuse?

Now, for each current PBD member, identify the type of influence this person has. I have used the word *influence* here and not *help* because some of the people on your current board might not be all that helpful. In fact, some of them might have a negative influence on your performance and well-being. But because you have given them de facto power, whether you realize it or not, you have given them a place on your board. Now assess the kind of influence each person has. If your Butt Kicker or Cheerleader is really a critic, albeit an influential one, decide if that person should really remain on your board.

Establish Your New Board

WHEN YOU HAVE completed this task, you will have a list of the ideal board members you have selected from the archetypes presented in this chapter and those you have chosen to add. You will also have a list of your current board members by name and by the positive or negative impact each has on you. Now match the two lists. Note that some people might actually perform more than one task. For example, my Problem Solver is also a Cheerleader, yet I still have another person as the Cheerleader. It's theoretically possible to have a one-person board who represents many different archetypes, but this is highly unlikely. Such a person might be able to provide the insights and advice from the perspective of each of the basic archetypes, but such people are rare indeed.

My Current Board of Directors

From the list you created earlier, enter the names of the people you allow to have influence over you:

Name	Category of Member (e.g., Problem Solver, Butt Kicker, Politician, etc.)

How do your two lists match? For those current members who fit nicely into your ideal board, no problem. For those ideal member slots that are not filled, who do you know who would be willing to sign up for those roles? What about the people who don't fit any of the ideal positions? These are the people you will want to excuse from your PBD.

PBD FAQs

AS YOU GO about the creation of your ideal board, here are several Frequently Asked Questions (FAQs) you may want to consider.

Q: Do I have to formally ask each member to be on my board?

A: No. But in most cases it would be helpful. This is particularly important if you expect this person to do something or invest time and energy on your behalf. If you have silent expectations that go unshared with your board member, you are likely to be disappointed. On the other hand, my Cheerleader is my wife, and I have never formerly asked her to be on my board.

Q: How do I go about actually asking someone to be on my board?

A: There are several steps:

1. *Get clear on what exactly you want your prospective board member to do.* The more explicit you can be the better. For example, rather than just saying, "Be my Problem Solver," you might say, "I really respect your ability to define and solve problems. I'd love to be able to come to you when I hit a roadblock to get perspectives on how to handle it. This could be in person or over the phone and, of course, only when you have the time to help."

2. *Contact your prospective board member and ask for support.* First explain the concept of your PBD and explain the role you wish him or her to play. It is important to acknowledge that this is a purely voluntary relationship and whatever obligations are incurred by either of you come from a sincere desire to help. It is best if you actually make it easy for this individual to say no to your request. If you do this, then you will know that when you get a yes, it is sincere and not out of a sense of obligation.

3. *Establish ground rules that will guide the relationship.* This is an important step in aligning expectations. A good way to start is to ask your prospective board member what reservations or concerns, if any, he or she has. Also ask what would be the best way to secure his or her help. For example, are there any times when it would be inappropriate to call this person for guidance? If the person's job or

personal life will limit effectiveness, it is good to find this out at the beginning.

4. *Make it clear that it's understood that either person may need to step away from the partnership for any reason at any time.* This gives both you and, more important, your board member an easy out in the future. And you should plan to take the initiative and be an advocate on your own behalf. Any initiative that comes from your board member will be a great bonus.

Q: What about personal problems and issues?

A: This board is established for your professional well-being. It will be most effective if personal issues not related to your work are avoided. You are not asking a board member to be therapist but rather a job/career advisor.

Q: What if I have a special short-term situation for which I could use some advice, but my board may not have the required expertise?

A: There is no reason why you can't create an ad hoc board specifically chosen to help you through an unexpected transition. When I left my company after twenty-eight years to set up my own speaking business, I asked four people to be on a temporary Transition Board of Directors. One of those four had also left the company after sixteen years. She would not normally be someone I turned to for counsel and advice, but her insight into changing jobs was essential to me during the transition.

This is the opportunity for you to put Pogo's words "None of us is as smart as all of us" into action. You can achieve this when you *Get connected at work, identify your Personal Board of Directors, and then assemble your board.* When you do this you will have taken a big step in mastering the interconnectedness that has become a cornerstone of contemporary business success. You will have established a network of people who want and are willing to help you to succeed. With their help, the odds of your doing so are just that much greater.

Action Steps

BASED ON THE information and exercises in this chapter what actions will you begin to take to get out of your own way?

- I will start . . .

- I will stop . . .

- I will do more . . .

- I will do less . . .

- I will do differently . . .

Be Yourself

*The single most important thing you can do in business
is to be yourself.*

—Sherry Lansing,
CEO, Paramount Pictures

I N THE POPULAR movie *Jerry Maguire*, the hero—a sports attorney
unhappy with his work—has an epiphany at 1 A.M. He realizes that he
has lost touch with his first love . . . the people he serves, the athletes.
And in the process he has lost himself as well.

Maguire creates a mission statement in which he spills his guts about
how the business of business hardened his humanity and turned him
into an actor saying only what people want to hear for the sake of his
"success." The importance of speaking this truth hit him when the
twelve-year-old son of a client asked him what it was he stood for. It was
the look on that child's face when he had no answer that kept Jerry up
that evening, crafting the mission statement that would get him fired.

It was the look on another's child's face that set another, real-life high-
powered attorney—Ric Giardina—on a similar self-quest for meaning
and authenticity at work. Giardina was one of two principal architects

of the "Intel Inside" branding campaign—a remarkable marketing strat-egy that more than doubled name recognition of Intel by home-PC buyers in just two years.[1] In exchange for co-packaging with the "Intel Inside" logo, computer manufacturers were given a generous advertising allowance.

Ric orchestrated the massive worldwide rollout and it worked beau-tifully, but it came at huge personal cost to his time, energy, and iden-tity. In Giardina's words, "I was living from garage to garage and in two different worlds with two different faces: the Corporate Ric and the *Real* Ric." And Corporate Ric was destroying his counterpart at home.

You at Work and You at Home

BECAUSE IT WAS always morning somewhere in the Intel world, Cor-porate Ric was always on call and had to be ready to field a crisis at any moment. His game face stayed on longer and longer at home, so long in fact that his daughter reacted:

> As usual, I just spent the 45-minute ride home on the phone with the Asian and European offices because their days were just beginning. My head was still buzzing with all of that when I walked in and said, "Daddy's home." My daughter stopped dead in her tracks about four feet away from me and stared without a trace of recognition. And then she lost it. For twenty or thirty seconds while she cried wildly, I just froze. I stared at her trying to analyze the situation, as if she was another problem employee. My wife charged into the room, swooped her into her arms, and soothed her with words that would forever change the way I worked and the way I viewed work: "It's okay. Daddy's in his work mode. He'll be back in a little while."

It was at that moment that Ric realized he had become two distinct people. After some soul-searching, he understood how domineering his corporate persona had become, leaving little room for the real one. He realized that, at his core, he was "the compassionate type, not the 'manly' type." Says Ric, "When I clicked into Corporate Ric, I naturally drew from my army experiences and became *that* instead of the warm and fuzzy people-person type that I naturally am." He decided that from that moment forward, no more schizophrenia. He would just simply be himself. He fully expected to be fired. So be it.

Living in Present Time

AFTER TWENTY-FIVE YEARS with Intel, Ric was fluent in business-speak, in thinking one thing and saying another, in acting one way at home and another at work. But the next day at work it was all going to end. It was all going to be real. Giardina vowed that from then on he would live in "present time," really listening to each person, regardless of who they were, as if he were talking to the most important person on earth. Ric decided to be consciously grateful and celebratory, to lighten up and keep everything in perspective. He would tell the absolute, un-cushioned truth, no matter the cost, no matter how inconsequential or how painful.

Instead of getting fired, Ric blossomed, as did the people who worked for him. His authenticity was not only attractive to superiors, it also attracted talented people to work for him. Says Ric, "It was because they could be who they were around me, and that is the ultimate competitive advantage."

Be Yourself

WHEN YOU CONSIDER the phrase "be yourself," it has subtle but important meaning. The simple statement, "Be yourself," means owning yourself in your current state of being, the amazingly great and the not so good; the genius part you discovered in chapter 4, "Get Out of Your Own Way," *and* the part that is a bumbler.

In many ways, mastering the ability to *be yourself* is the most challenging of the Six Ways of Being, but what makes it so worthwhile is that the more progress you make the less baggage you bear. When your load is lightened your relationship with workmates improves, your productivity increases, and you find more ways to experience joy in your work. Nothing is more freeing than total self-acceptance. So if you're consciously or unconsciously straining under the unnecessary burden of an idealized "you," this way of being will help you unload it.

At work, as in life, there are basically two kinds of people: those who remain true to themselves regardless of circumstances, and those who are ready to change—depending on perceived expectations. The routes to getting real, to being yourself, are distinctly personal, but three can help get you there:

1. Speak your truth.
2. Lighten up.
3. Be your own best friend.

SPEAK YOUR TRUTH

Sacred cows make the best hamburger.

BOB KRIEGEL,
Inner Skiing

THERE IS A classic training video for business called *The Abilene Paradox*. In it a group of family and friends are sitting around doing pretty much of nothing. Finally one person suggests that they all go to Abilene, a trip that would take a couple of hours by car. While no one really reacts enthusiastically to the suggestion, they all pile into the car and head off to the city. As it turns out, they have a terrible time. They are bored and feel as though the entire trip was a huge waste of time. They argue about what possessed them to go in the first place.

When the griping finally subsides, it seems that no one, not a single person, actually wanted to go to Abilene, but they all consented to go and had a horrible time. The question is: How did this debacle happen? Who was to blame? The answer is that they were all to blame. Each person was responsible because he or she did not weigh the options, make a choice, and state a preference clearly and unequivocally. It was a "group-think" phenomenon where everyone went along with everyone else.

The Abilene Paradox is a simple story that derives its power from its accurate reflection of what really goes on in many companies. Too often, when it comes time to take a stand, to tell the truth, we bail out. Best Buy, the nation's number one consumer electronics retailer, has spent over $10 million on executive coaching for all sixty-seven corporate officers over the past several years. The work has included every senior manager from vice presidents up to Richard Schulze, the CEO and founder. One of the reasons for the coaching was that these veteran executives realized that they were not speaking with younger managers in a candid way. In other words, they weren't telling the truth. By their own admission, they lacked the time and the guts.

"True" Success

IF THOMAS JEFFERSON was right when he said, "Honesty is the first chapter in the book of wisdom," what happens when we do not tell the truth? Like the people in *The Abilene Paradox*, time and effort are wasted, fools' ventures are pursued, and people become bored, dispirited, angry, and sometimes even hostile.

One of the characteristics of highly successful organizations is that diverse opinions are welcome. There are no sacred cows. Anything is challengeable and, indeed, in this atmosphere, people will challenge.

Diversity can be golden. Research shows that a highly diverse workforce will be more productive than one that is largely homogeneous. According to a *Wall Street Journal* article, "Companies that are successful in encouraging diversity are also more likely to see higher stock values."[2] Why? Because the naturally differing points of view of these diverse groups create an amalgam of important variables to be considered—and this stimulates dynamic creativity.

If truth telling is so important why don't we see it more in organizations? There are a number of reasons. Perhaps the most prominent are fear of punishment, fear of looking stupid, and not being asked.

Fear of Punishment

IN RESEARCHING *CUSTOMER-CENTERED GROWTH*, my coauthor, Diane Hessan, and I talked to more than two hundred companies on six different continents. One of the questions asked was, "What word or phrase best describes the culture of your company?" I was astonished at how often the word fear came up. With all the current economic changes, people are cautious. Popular and apparently productive long-term employees are downsized and more and more jobs are being structured as consultant free-agent positions. Job security is a thing of the past. The work climate favors a "keep-your-head-down" mentality.

Based on research originally conducted in Japan, the diagram on page 188, "The Iceberg of Ignorance," represents an apt description of the impact of fear on organizations today.[3]

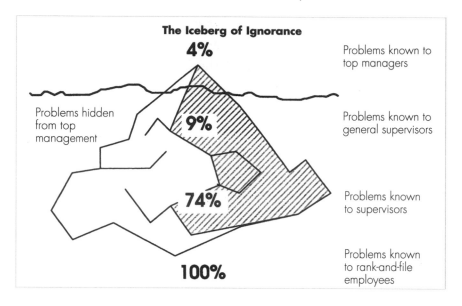

The Iceberg of Ignorance

4% — Problems known to top managers

Problems hidden from top management

9% — Problems known to general supervisors

74% — Problems known to supervisors

100% — Problems known to rank-and-file employees

As a group, front-line, lower-level employees are aware of 100 percent of an organization's problems. As you move up the hierarchy, 74 percent of the problems are known at the supervisory level. But look what happens at the next level. The percentage of known problems drops from 74 to 9 percent—an astonishing decline. One probable reason for the drop-off is that bad news doesn't travel up the hierarchy. After all, when the messenger gets shot, the messages stop.

When front-line personnel are afraid to report problems, a company is plagued by costly and wasteful glitches that persist without resolution. For example, until the folks in the trenches spoke up, publisher Boardroom, Inc., was paying premium postage to ship books that weighed four pounds. CEO Martin Edelston looked into an employee suggestion that they find a way to avoid such an expense and discovered that by slicing just ⅛ of an inch off each book, they would save over $1.5 million a year.[4]

If you have seen colleagues lose their jobs, bonuses, or promotions for speaking up or telling the truth, or have experienced this yourself, you are in a toxic organizational environment and might consider changing managers, departments, or even organizations. If such incidents don't occur, check your level of truth telling and see if more is appropriate.

Where Does Your Organization Stand?

To what extent do you believe people in your company are comfortable being themselves? Check the one that applies:

☐	People expend great energy creating false fronts that they believe others want to see.
☐	Sometimes people can express who they really are, but it pays to be cautious.
☐	People are pretty closed off. Only when they trust you will they really "show themselves."
☐	People are generally pretty genuine and will let you know who they are.
☐	No problem. People show up as they are and this diversity of personality, style, and opinion is welcomed, even celebrated.

What would need to change for people to feel comfortable? For you to feel comfortable?

Fear of Looking Stupid

ANOTHER REASON PEOPLE are reluctant to speak the truth is that they're afraid of appearing stupid. This tends to occur more in autocratic organizations where the "boss" is the one with all the answers. For example, one professional services firm held a three-day meeting of its entire professional staff. The purpose was to review the numbers, learn about new products, and participate in professional development sessions. One of these sessions was designed to teach the staff about dialogue—a highly effective communications process built on the work of MIT physicist David Bohm. Led by a facilitator, groups of ten people tackled the question of how they felt about truth telling in their own organization.

Because managers were not mixed with the people they managed—and because the facilitators were from outside the company—people did indeed tell the truth about telling the truth. They discovered many people had quit trying to speak up because they felt their managers regarded opinions they didn't agree with as frivolous and not relevant. Leaders quite unconsciously had suppressed people's willingness to offer opinions and suggest improvements. At the end of the day, people just didn't want to take the risk of feeling stupid even though, deep down, they believed their points of view could be helpful to the organization they served.

So how do you go about expressing the truth so that your managers and colleagues listen and weigh your opinions? One way is to acknowledge other opinions and express what is true for *you* rather than what is *true* for the universe.

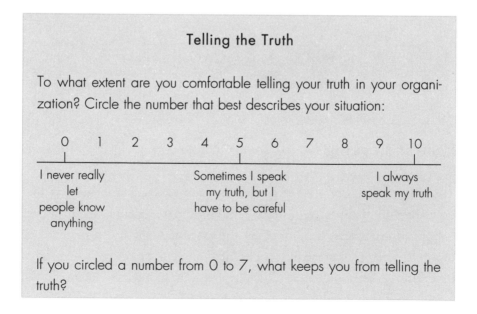

Telling the Truth

To what extent are you comfortable telling your truth in your organization? Circle the number that best describes your situation:

```
0    1    2    3    4    5    6    7    8    9    10
|                        |                        |
I never really      Sometimes I speak        I always
let                 my truth, but I        speak my truth
people know         have to be careful
anything
```

If you circled a number from 0 to 7, what keeps you from telling the truth?

Listen and Be Heard

THERE ARE TWO practices that will help you communicate your opinion in a way that can be heard. Surprisingly, the first has nothing to do with talking. It is how you listen. By listening effectively you earn the right to speak and to be listened to. The key to listening well is to be present—listening with the intent of modifying your opinion based on what is being presented.

When you enter a conversation, insistent on your opinion, you listen defensively. While the other person is talking, you aren't listening—you are thinking about how you will counterattack. And when the other person is listening defensively too, no communication takes place, time is wasted, little is accomplished, and poor decisions result. David Pottruck, president and co-chief executive of Charles Schwab, understands this phenomenon when he, in his words, "listens to hear rather than to answer."[5] When he does this, Schwab employees confide in him and tell him what's really going on inside his company. With this more accurate picture he makes better informed decisions for his customers, shareholders, and most important, for his employees.

I have actually witnessed business meetings that looked and sounded more like college debates or oratorical warfare than a sensible discussion of alternatives. It is sometimes as though people actually try to "win" a meeting. This is nonsense. The point is not to "win." The point is to arrive at the best decision possible.

Open versus Closed Listening

1. Think of the last time you were in a meeting or discussing differing points of view with a coworker. What was going on in your mind when the other person was talking? Were you sincerely trying to understand this person's point of view or loading up for a counterattack?

2. Write a one-sentence version of a colleague's opinion.
3. Write a one-sentence version of your response.
4. What type of listening led to your response? What response would you have made if you incorporated your coworker's opinion in your thinking?

"My" Truth, Not "the" Truth

THE SECOND PRACTICE to help you communicate your opinions effectively signals to your "audience" that you are not presenting an absolute truth but rather your thoughtful perspective. Before you offer your opinion at a meeting, acknowledge the boundaries of your expertise. At the meeting, you can express this—as well as respect for your colleagues—by prefacing your opinions with phrases such as *"What's true for me is . . ." "It seems to me . . ." "The way I see it is. . . ."* When you believe that you are speaking *your* truth these short phrases inform the listener that you are offering an opinion based on your previous listening and expertise and are open to modification.

Speaking Your Truth

1. Identify an opinion that you want to express at an upcoming meeting.
2. What experience/knowledge are you drawing upon in forming this opinion?
3. Identify other types of experience or knowledge that could lead to a different opinion. Acknowledge the boundaries of your own knowledge/experience, but don't dismiss your opinion.
4. When you express your opinion, preface it with "What is true for me is . . ." or a similar disclaimer.
5. See if you notice any difference in the way colleagues receive your

opinions. Also notice if others who express themselves forcefully create resistance to their opinions?

Even with the best intentions to communicate fairly and purely, things can go awry. If you find yourself frustrated even when you're listening and speaking your truth, look for decision-making patterns in your department or company that will limit your ability to participate. These include (1) abdication—when no decision is made, or decisions are jettisoned as soon as employees leave the rooms; (2) dictation—when your manager or another person in power makes all the decisions; and (3) compromise—when opinions are combined to placate egos rather than to find the best position.

When decision making is effective, a fourth mode of reaching a decision will be in play: confrontation. While it may sound a bit aggressive, confrontation is nothing more than discussing problems and opportunities with candor based on preset evaluation criteria, respect for the other person's point of view, and the intention of doing what is best for the organization. When this mode is used, you will feel comfortable listening to other opinions, understanding differences, and finding a position that best serves your company—whether it is based on your opinion or not. When you are able to exhibit full enthusiasm for decisions that are not based on your opinions, it is usually because deep down you trust that your point of view has been heard and seriously considered.

How Are Decisions Made in Your Company?

In the chart below, enter your best guess as to the percentage of decisions you believe are made using each mode of decision making. Of course, you don't know for sure, but give your best estimate. The total of the four modes should add up to 100%.

MODE	%
1. Abdicate	_____
2. Dictate	_____
3. Compromise	_____
4. Confront	_____
	Total: 100%

Now, think about decisions you make in one-on-one meetings with your manager. Again, estimate the percentage of decisions that are made using each mode. How can you shift the percentage more toward confrontation? To what extent does the company culture support you in confronting decision issues?

Not Asked

THE THIRD AND perhaps most obvious reason people don't speak their truth is that no one asks them what they think. Consider the following sentiments expressed by a midlevel manager at a communications company:

There's little reaching out to a broad array of employees for input here. Although I have lots of ideas about how this company could use the Internet more effectively, I'm not in the decision-making inner circle and don't know how to approach them.

Regrettably, this employee's situation is not unusual. According to research conducted with front-line service providers who had left their companies, the number one reason they gave for leaving was "nobody asks me what I think."

Michael Bonsignore, chairman and CEO of Honeywell International, sees it in a similar way when he asks: "How can you be a world-class company if your people are intimidated about speaking freely? At the end of the day, my employees may be the only sustainable competitive advantage that we have."

To put action behind these sentiments, Bonsignore spends two days per week traveling to Honeywell plants where he mixes with employees at all levels and elicits their ideas. He holds "town meetings" with large groups of employees and routinely meets with smaller groups as well. He says, "Since no other executive but me is present at those small meetings, there's an atmosphere of candor, and a chance to get a unique perspective I would never get if I stayed in my office."[6]

LIGHTEN UP

Not a shred of evidence exists in favor of the idea that life is serious.

— BRENDAN GILL

THE SOUTHWEST AIRLINES flight from San Francisco was without incident, a normal commute at the end of a successful business day. With little more than a modest jolt, the wheels met tarmac, and we were on the ground and heading toward the arrival gate. Then, suddenly, the brakes kicked in, and a hundred or so passengers lurched against their seat belts. At this point the unbelievable happened. The pilot yelled over the P.A. system, "Whoa, Nellie, whoa!" For a moment I didn't know whether I was in a stagecoach or a 737.

Everyone on the plane broke up laughing. The pilot was clearly enjoying himself and it was infectious. And why not? Who says we can't have a little fun as we go about our business or as we go about the business of living our lives? As it turns out, this kind of merriment is not uncommon on Southwest flights. Attendants make the perfunctory preflight announcements in a Donald Duck voice or hide in the overhead bins to surprise the unsuspecting passenger storing a briefcase. Where do they get off pulling antics like this? Well, it might just come from their wacky founder and CEO Herb Kelleher who himself has been known to ride his Harley-Davidson motorcycle into Southwest's headquarters.

This absolute dedication to lightening up is one of the reasons Southwest always ranks very high in *Fortune*'s annual list of the top 100 companies to work for. Starting with their CEO, everyone in the company has permission to have fun. As one Southwest employee said, "They respect you, empower you, use your ideas and encourage you to be yourself." In addition to winning the U.S. Department of Transportation's Triple Crown service award each year, no other airline has been as profitable as Southwest, which has made money every year since 1973—an amazing feat in a highly competitive and capital-intensive industry.

Act Light

THERE IS A learning model developed by the Sterling Institute to train entrepreneurs: it's the Think, Talk, Act model. The institute found that if people could be trained to *think* like an entrepreneur, *talk* like an entrepreneur, and, finally, *act* like an entrepreneur, lo and behold, pretty soon you would actually have an entrepreneur. The same is true for lightening up.

Norman Cousins was cruising along through life when the bad news hit. He was diagnosed with spinal arthritis, a chronic and degenerative disease. Traditional procedures for treating this disease were not 100 percent successful, so Cousins decided to create his own therapy. He decided to literally laugh it off. He secured videotapes of classic movie comedies and reruns of television comedy specials. He reasoned that the more he laughed the better he would get and his Rx actually worked.

Dr. Madan Kataria, a physician from India, explains how the Cousins therapy works. It can be traced back to an ancient yogic breathing posture and is an aerobic exercise where oxygen levels in the body increase. He says, "There is a greater exchange of oxygen when you laugh. It is food for the cells of your body." With this comes better circulation over the entire body, reduced blood pressure, improved sleep, and less stress.

Today, companies sponsor some 150 laughter clubs around India. One of country's largest engineering firms, for example, encourages executives to leave the office at lunchtime en masse and, on the sidewalk outside of their office building, engage in fifteen minutes of rigorous frivolity.

The laughing ritual provides physical as well as emotional improvements. Pushpa Goenka, a social worker, says, "If I start my day with a laugh, my whole outlook changes." Jyoti Varma, a fifty-five-year-old mother of three, says, "I used to have pain in my knees, pains in my neck, but they are now gone. My whole outlook on life has changed."

Laughter is contagious. Says Kataria, "I may laugh for no reason, but you, seeing me, will also laugh. When I see you laugh, I will laugh in response." Danish comedian Victor Borge understood this happy viral phenomenon when he said, "Laughter is the shortest distance between two people."

Lighten Up about Yourself

WE ALL HAVE stories that prove Murphy's Law: If anything can go wrong it will. My experience with Mr. Murphy is that he is a sadist. In other words, he doesn't just show up, he seems to hold off his unpleasant intrusions until the exact point when you are most exposed and vulnerable.

When Murphy strikes, one of the best things you can do is to enjoy the practical joke and laugh at yourself. It breaks the tension and creates recovery time. It relaxes you by getting you to breathe, loosen your muscles, and ease your mind. It holds back your tendency to self-criticize. It puts the people around you at ease and lets them know that you are aware of the mistake and recognize that it isn't fatal. It minimizes the error and builds the confidence of others that you are not thrown by it. It reflects your humility and humanness. Few people enjoy being around someone who projects a facade of perfection—until they see them actually make an error.

When you are able to laugh at your errors, people are more than willing to show compassion and laugh with you because it puts them in touch with their own fallibility. At these times we hear people say things like, "Well, you're only human," or "Better you than me."

Laugh at Yourself

HOW READILY ARE you able to laugh at yourself? Think of three of the most embarrassing mistakes you have created at work. When they occurred were you able to laugh at yourself? If not, why not? How about six months later? Imagine that a colleague—not you—committed the error. How would you help him or her find humor in the mistake?

Laughter as a Success Factor

I BELIEVE THAT a company's success is directly related to the amount of laughter one hears in its meetings. For a number of years I had the privilege of serving on the executive committee of the Instructional Systems Association (ISA), a group of companies in the training industry whose membership continues to grow year in and year out since its founding in 1978. For many people, going to meetings is akin to walking the Bataan Death March. Mention the words *committee, task force,* and *board*, and eyes roll back and people frown. That's because, for the most part, internal business meetings are inefficient and poorly run. Maybe that's why Harvard economist John Kenneth Galbraith said, "Meetings are indispensable when you don't want to do anything."

But at the ISA sessions laughter ruled the day—our meetings were amazingly productive, efficient, timely, and most of all fun. We laughed at ourselves, our industry, and at circumstances in general, and that caused everyone to look forward to every meeting and the work we would accomplish. The relationships I built with those board members over the years remain strong to this day due to our ability to lighten up—a great resource when I'm looking for a network of support.

Lightening up is closely akin to truth telling. Court jesters were always the ones who told the king the truth because they were not bound by rigidity, by having to look "good." As fools, they had no such constraints. Having a touch of foolishness brings authenticity to your work and helps you keep your mistakes, your missteps, and your "tragedies" in perspective.

And, lightening up—speaking your truth in a way that makes the rest of us enjoy it—shows you have confidence in yourself, and displaying your confidence is the basis of respect from others.

BE YOUR OWN BEST FRIEND

Love the one you're with . . .

—CROSBY, STILLS, AND NASH

A MAJOR PREMISE of *Love the Work You're With* is that much of the satisfaction and joy we derive from work is due to what we do, not what is done to us. As discussed in the "Welcome" to this book, people often change jobs only to find the same problems resurface. It may very well be that the job you now have is a poor fit for your talents, ambitions, or values. What this book has tried to do is help you figure out how much of the problem is due to external circumstances and how much is due to your view of them. With that insight you can move on, if need be, fully confident that it is the job, not you, that is at issue.

No job or position, however, can provide any of the intangible rewards—such as esteem, trust, and respect—if you are not able to accept them. If you don't hold esteem for yourself, trust yourself, or respect yourself, surely you'll discount it when others do. When this happens, despite plenty of external rewards and accolades, you will never hit that sweet spot of job satisfaction.

To love the work you're with, then, starts with loving the one you're with—you. How do you achieve this? One helpful way is to think of it in terms of becoming your own best friend.

When are you most yourself in the presence of others? Probably when you are with really good friends. At these times, we let our hair down, share confidences, laugh at ourselves, expect the hard truth we need to hear, and trust that these comrades will stick up—and around—for us no matter what. Perhaps most important, we know that our friends have seen the best and worse we have to offer, and accept us anyway.

Similarly, when you are your own best friend at work, it is *you* who shows up regardless of the situation, not someone you think others want to see. The more you allow this authentic, fun, and self-confident core of you to shine, the more the creativity, joy, and can-do spirit is unleashed within yourself and within those at work.

So what is a best friend? A few common answers are someone who . . .

- really cares
- tells the truth
- supports and defends
- loves unconditionally

Let's look at each in the context of befriending yourself at work.

CARE FOR YOURSELF

"WHO CARES?" IS a phrase rarely spoken out loud, unless in anger, but is often a subtle message we get as we go about our work. Who cares *about you*, about how you feel if you blow the sale, miss the deadline, or are overwhelmed with responsibilities? A best friend will, even if no one else does.

Sometimes good friends are like good therapists. They have an uncanny ability to listen to us at several levels. They hear our words, they put these words in the context of other life events we have shared with them, and they hear the emotional content of whatever we are saying. Remember David Pottruck's philosophy of listening to understand rather than to answer? This is the way a best friend listens to you. They listen as if they are afraid to miss a word. They listen so well because they care.

If really listening is core to caring for another, what do you hear when you listen to yourself? Do you discount your own opinions as soon as they are challenged at a meeting? Do you hesitate to offer them? A friend would urge you to do so. Do you treat yourself and your own opinions the way you would treat a friend's? If not, or not often enough, here are some tools for treating yourself as well as you would a friend:

Listening to Oneself

1. The next time you are upset or agitated, find a private place and speak out loud what is going on in your mind. Listen to yourself as you would your best friend. What words, emotions, and personal history are making your feelings so powerful at this time? What inner voices, as discussed in chapter 4, "Get Out of Your Own Way," do you hear? Talk to yourself as if you were confiding in a good friend, all the while listening to find clues that can clarify issues, find an appropriate course of action, or gain a new perspective.

2. An even better method of listening to yourself is to tape-record your outburst, listen to the tape, and pause it to interrupt with questions as would a friend. At this time you are literally outside of yourself, being your own best friend. You will be amazed at how many issues you can handle this way.

Another aspect of caring is "to take care of yourself." When you hear someone say that she or he takes care of her- or himself what immediately comes to mind? Self-respect? Probably. Taking care of yourself can be evidenced in myriad ways—such as in the time, expense, and interest you invest in your physical appearance, health, and personal growth—and it says to you and others, "I'm worth the effort."

Describe Your Best Friend

Take a moment to answer this question: When you think of your best friend, what attributes do you appreciate most? List them below, and in the opposite column describe how you can convert that attribute into one you can use to befriend yourself.

My best friend is a person who . . .	As my own best friend, I am a person who . . .

Show Yourself You Care

BEST FRIENDS THINK we deserve the world. How can you exhibit that same kind of self-care? Make a list of all those little things you would like to do for yourself but hesitate for reasons of time, money, or feeling too self-indulgent. Is it a really nice pen? A new gadget for the office? Holding your calls for a five-minute relaxation break? Pick just one that you can do and do it. Keep this list active by jotting down new "extravagances" as they come to mind. When you feel it's time to do something nice for yourself, open up your list as if it's a box of candy treats and pick one.

TELL YOURSELF THE TRUTH

EARLIER IN THIS chapter we discussed truth telling. The focus, of course, was your ability and willingness to tell the truth to others. When you are your own best friend this ability turns inward and you speak your own truth to yourself. When you are able to do this you can identify the many places and circumstances when you are likely to stop yourself from moving forward at work. Two questions that will be helpful here are: "What are my faulty assumptions?" and "What are my limiting beliefs?"

We often take inappropriate action based on faulty assumptions we hold. For example, you neglect to send out an agenda to the meeting ahead of time because you *assume* everyone should know what the meeting is about when, in reality, they don't. Or, you don't ask for a raise because you *assume* there's no budget for it and your manager won't give it to you even if there were.

Limiting beliefs are like faulty assumptions. They are what we hold to be true that keeps us from reaching top performance levels and achieving what we would like to achieve at work. Before Roger Bannister ran the first four-minute mile there was a limiting belief that this was beyond the reach of man. Once he shattered this limiting belief, a host of other runners followed suit and ran the mile in less than four minutes. I have seen the same phenomenon in sales organizations. Every salesperson knows what the biggest sale to date is in his or her organization. Like the four-minute mile, the last largest sale sits out there waiting to be broken. And when someone comes along and surpasses it, say, by another 30 percent, sure enough, other orders of that magnitude will soon follow.

Debunking Faulty Assumptions and Limiting Beliefs

HOCKEY GREAT WAYNE Gretzky said that you miss 100 percent of the shots you don't take. Faulty assumptions and limiting beliefs keep us from taking our best "shots" at business. On a piece of paper, list the faulty assumptions and limiting beliefs that are holding you back at work. Now, how can you eliminate them so they will not throw you off track? Naming them will require that you be truthful with yourself.

Best friends keep us honest. Sometimes they put a finger in our face and say, "You know what? You're going the wrong way." They love us enough to make us uncomfortable about those behaviors and attitudes that are ultimately self-defeating. Consider having the courage to do the same — to tell the hard truth to yourself about yourself — by taking a "fearless moral inventory" as is done by those in Alcoholics Anonymous. Look at yourself as a best friend would — with unconditional acceptance as well as brutal honesty — to discover those behaviors and attitudes that are hurtful to yourself, others, and your career; and identify steps that you can take to make appropriate changes.

Take Inventory

IMAGINE THAT YOU have asked a good friend at work to give you feedback and give it to you straight. What would he or she say about your interpersonal skills? Your motivation? Your business accumen? Your know-how? What would you do well to change?

SUPPORT YOURSELF

A BEST FRIEND is also one who unfailingly shows up in a crisis. When you feel as if your castle at work, whatever it may be, is being stormed and the walls are about to fall in on you, it is your best friend who magically shows up, often without having been asked. Similarly, when you are your own best friend you are able to show up and assert yourself.

John had a habit of not doing this. In dealing with the powerful people at work, he had the habit of undermining himself. He would make a beautifully assertive statement, full of confidence and clarity and then lose it all with a tentative and meek sounding tag line like, "Don't you think?" or "But then again, I could be wrong." What was happening here is that John didn't have the self-confidence to keep from deflating his own balloon. He couldn't show up for himself by stepping into his power and retain it in the midst of a crisis or challenging situation.

Claiming Your Power

IN TIMES OF crisis or great challenge at work, what do you do to undermine yourself? How can you avoid it?

LOVE YOURSELF UNCONDITIONALLY

AN ARABIAN PROVERB creates a wonderful picture of what being your own best friend might look like:

> A friend is one to whom one may pour out all the contents of one's heart, chaff and grain together, knowing that the gentlest of hands will take and sift it, keep what is worth keeping and with a breath of kindness blow the rest away.

When you think about yourself, are you "gentle," and do you trust that, day in and day out, you will keep what is worth keeping and "with a breath of kindness blow the rest away"? For most people, unfortunately, the answer is no.

I have asked hundreds of people this simple question: *Do you love yourself unconditionally?* I estimate that fewer than 10 percent of the respondents say yes. About 30 percent say no. That leaves roughly 60 percent who put themselves in no-man's-land and offer some kind of qualifier to their answer. They will say things like: "Some of the time" or "I'm getting there" or "On the good days."

For those who say "no" or "sometimes," I ask a follow-up question: *What would have to change for you to answer yes?* When it comes to what would need to be different at work, I hear the following:

- "If I could make over six figures, then I would love myself."
- "If I could finish that M.B.A. I would be able to love myself."
- "If I were younger and could avoid the mistakes I made early in my career, I'd love myself."

People go to great lengths to find ways to avoid loving themselves. The most common—like the ones stated above—have to do with internal barriers to self-love. Some, like being younger, are beyond your control and aren't going to happen. If they become a condition for accepting yourself, then it simply won't happen.

Another sort of answer arises when I ask my follow-up question. Typically, work-related responses go something like this:

- "When my boss sees my true potential."
- "When I earn the respect of my peers, I'll know I'm worthy."
- "When my name is known in my industry."

These are external barriers that often involve someone else. As in the examples here, someone else has to acknowledge you in some way before you will acknowledge yourself. The trap, of course, is that your self-validation has to come from another source and when it doesn't, as in the example of being younger above, accepting yourself will not happen.

MAKING UNCONDITIONAL DECISIONS

LOOKING AT YOUR answers to these questions might make you uncomfortable as you begin to see how hard you are on yourself. It's time to undermine the rationale for not accepting yourself: *When you're asked whether you love yourself unconditionally or not, who decides the answer?*

Of course the answer is "you." As long as you're deciding, why not decide to love yourself unconditionally? Such a decision will go a long way to support you in your career. On a pragmatic level, it translates into accepting your strengths and weaknesses, investing in your personal and professional development, and getting out of work environments that are stifling your happiness, creativity, productivity, or health. Living such a decision is not instantaneous or easy. You will slip back into old habits — but it can pay significant dividends. John Seely Brown, vice president and chief scientist at Xerox Corporation, understood this well when he said, "The real challenge today is unlearning . . . each of us has a 'mental model' that we've used to make sense of the world. The harder you fight to hold on to specific assumptions, the more likely there's gold in letting go of them."[7]

Self-Compassion

1. On a piece of paper identify three things you can do starting right now to love yourself unconditionally.

2. Now record three things you can do to have more compassion for yourself when you are about to lambaste yourself. How can you head off such self-mugging before it gains momentum?

YOU AS A CATALYST

EARLY IN THIS chapter I said that to *be yourself* is perhaps the most challenging of the Six Ways of Being to master. We are creatures of habit and for many of us the habits we call work patterns have been ingrained over many years. It is these patterns that often keep us from being able to speak our truth, lighten up, and be our own best friend. To break them with such new behaviors can feel risky at times. But the risk of putting *yourself* out there is worth it.

Action Steps

BASED ON THE information and exercises in this chapter, complete the following:

- I will start . . .

- I will stop . . .

- I will do more . . .

- I will do less . . .

- I will do differently . . .

Leader's Guide: How to Create a Spirited Workforce

What you need to run a business is optimism, humanism, enthusiasm, intuition, curiosity, love, humor, magic, and fun.

—ANITA RODDICK,
founder, The Body Shop

THE CHANGING ECONOMY of the last decade has created the need for a different kind of leadership, one that will challenge everyone up and down the hierarchy who has the responsibility for creating a high-performance work team.

The factors are there: the flattening of organizations, ever-widening spans of control, distributed and free-agent workforces, a more diverse age range of active workers, and a distinctly lower trust in management and leadership. The old and revered "command and control" leadership practices are simply no longer effective and a more participative approach is demanded. Several studies confirm that when a company adopts such an approach, good things happen: employees are delighted and this translates to eye-popping business results. Compared with traditional "command and control" companies, participative companies, on average, generate 200 percent more patents,[1] 500 percent more revenue, 800 percent more profit, 1,200 percent greater stock price, and $15,000 to $60,000 more market valuation per employee.[2]

As we observe the leaders in these highly successful enterprises, one common attitude seems to stand out. They believe a major priority is to establish the kind of culture that facilitates superior individual and group performance. They see themselves as environment creators and understand that when the proper climate is established, it will become a powerful multiplier of individual performance. Skip LeFauve clearly understood this when he put the fledgling Saturn Corporation on the map. He said, "My job is to create the kind of environment where individual excellence can emerge." He did, and Saturn produced levels of customer delight unparalleled in the tough automotive industry, an industry viewed with great cynicism and distrust.

Based on this insight, a reasonable definition of leadership for today is:

> To create an environment where people are willing and able to carry out the vision and strategy of the organization.

Further observation indicates that we face a crisis in leadership, since many others in these powerful positions are reluctant to follow suit and adapt to the requirements of the day. They continue operating with outdated and inappropriate assumptions about their employees. This leads to ineffective or, worse, negative leadership practices that alienate the very people who have to "get the work done." Today's incredibly high turnover is not just the by-product of a strong economy and dot-com companies raiding large corporations. It is directly related to inattentive leaders.

In a survey conducted by the Conference Board—an organization of business leaders—650 CEOs reported that their number-one issue was customer loyalty and the second most critical issue was "engaging employees in the company's vision and values." Bain & Company reports that chief executives are most confident in "strategy development" (85 percent), less so for "strategy implementation" (40 percent), and are not confident at all in the "alignment of people" (10 percent). When the Conference Board examined ratings of leadership capabilities to meet today's challenges, they discovered that only 8 percent of the respondents rated these abilities as "excellent" while 39 percent rated themselves as "fair" or "poor." Executive consultant and author Tracy Goss reflected on this leadership gap when she said: "Today's business leaders are reinventing everything but themselves. Unless executives realize that they must change not just what they do, but who they are, not just their sense of task, but their sense of themselves, they will fail."

So how do you bring the Six Ways of Being that we have discussed in this book into your organization? Three approaches will get you moving in the right direction:

1. Live the six ways.
2. Be vulnerable.
3. Be a cheerleader.

If you would like additional insight into your leadership strengths and areas to develop consider completing the twelve-question leadership self-assessment on page 227.

What Is Your Intention?

BEFORE INTRODUCING THE Six Ways of Being into your work unit, it will be helpful for you to examine your level of dedication. Intention is a powerful mobilizer of motivation and action. If your intent is not strong enough to adopt the Six Ways of Being and make them an integral part of your life and the life of your organization, you will not be able to lead by example. You may choose to discount the Six Ways of Being or you may opt to embrace and internalize some or all of them.

If you discount them, don't waste your time asking your employees to consider them. Your lack of investment will be obvious and you will risk confusing, or, even worse, disillusioning, your employees.

Test Your Intent

1. If you haven't already taken the self-assessment diagnostic at the beginning of this book, do so now. If you took it earlier, review your answers and the areas in which you will focus your efforts.
2. Identify how each Way of Being could enhance your work group's performance. How will it affect the bottom line? How will it affect morale?
3. Circle the number that best reflects your intent in the statement: "Bringing some or all of the Six Ways of Being into my work group is . . .

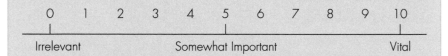

| 0 | 1 | 2 | 3 | 4 | 5 | 6 | 7 | 8 | 9 | 10 |

Irrelevant   Somewhat Important   Vital

Analysis: If you have circled a number below 8, your intent is probably not strong enough to support the work required to establish the Six Ways of Being. Either abandon this as a leadership approach or determine what you have to do to strengthen your intent. Review the payoffs to your work group. Consider any consequences of not developing each Way of Being.

LIVE THE SIX WAYS

An example isn't the main thing in influencing others, it's the only thing.

— ALBERT SCHWEITZER

THE FIRST RULE of leadership is lead by example. Gandhi understood this when he said, "You have to be what you want to see." When Sir Colin Marshall was first appointed as CEO of struggling British Airways some years ago, this champion of impeccable customer service led by example when, much to the astonishment of his employees, he actually showed up at Heathrow at 5:30 in the morning to greet passengers. Marilyn Carlson Nelson, head of the 180,000-person Carlson Companies, led by example when she Rollerbladed into a meeting of 4,000 employees to send a message about risk and nervousness. Herb Kelleher, the CEO of Southwest Airlines, led by example when he rolled up his sleeves and handled baggage during the busy Thanksgiving holiday. And John Chambers, who *Fortune* touts as the best CEO on earth, led the way when he insisted that his executives have the same 12- by 12-foot offices. What size is Chambers's office? 12- by 12-feet, of course.

Unfortunately, everyone doesn't automatically lead by example. According to Jeffery Pfeffer and Robert Sutton in their book, *The Knowing-Doing Gap*, "There is far more talk than action about using enlightened management techniques." Or as one CEO confided to me, "We don't really 'walk the talk' here. For us it's more like 'stumble the mumble.' "

Whether it is the Six Ways of Being or other values that you espouse for your group, once you are living them yourself—avoiding the "do as I say not as I do" syndrome of weak leadership—you are reinforcing those values in your group. A powerful way to think about bringing a new work culture to your group is to place your priorities on the following grid:

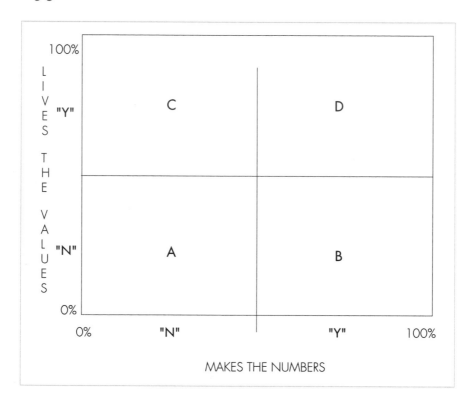

Think of a person in the work group you manage. To what extent does the person "make the numbers" and "live the values" you're encouraging? "Making the numbers," the horizontal axis, means the extent to which he or she usually meets performance targets. "Living the values" means the extent to which this person demonstrates the organization's core values as evidenced in his or her behavior. If your person is in box A, he or she is a drain. By not making the numbers he or she drains your performance and by not living the values he or she creates a drain on the culture of your work group. You must resolve this situation or the morale of the group will suffer. You may even have to consider removing this person from the team.

Your role model resides in box D. This is the superior performer who embodies the team's values. This is the person to be praised publicly, rewarded, and promoted. When you do this you are sending a message to the entire group that the way to get ahead is to be like this person.

The person in box C is your developmental project. His or her values are congruent with what you are encouraging—invested workers. The problem is with meeting quantitative goals. The action called for here is development. To assist you in pinpointing the problem you may want him or her to use the Performance Self-Analysis on page 130 to determine where to put his or her focus on development.

The biggest challenge is always the person who lives in box B. This is the abrasive high performer who makes the numbers but rejects your team values. For example, if "teamwork" is highly valued, what do you do about a top sales performer whose arrogance and self-serving behavior make it impossible for other members of the team to turn to him or her—or to get acknowledgment from the performer for their support? And what about the manager who berates and humiliates his or her people rather than respecting them and thereby flaunts the group's value of "respect for the individual"? As Jack Welch, the CEO of GE, says bluntly, "Making your numbers but not demonstrating our values is grounds for dismissal."[3] If such a person continues to flaunt the values, it is a major moment of truth for you, the leader. If you don't deal with it—and that probably means dismissing that person—you have signaled to your entire team that making the numbers is all-important and the values are worthless.

Reinforcing the Six Ways of Being

Beneath any or all of the following Six Ways of Being you wish to bring alive in your work group, list three actions you can do to make them a reality.

Follow Your Passion

1. _____
2. _____
3. _____

Be Home

1. _____
2. _____
3. _____

Create Your Own Reality

1. _____
2. _____
3. _____

Get Out of Your Own Way

1. _____
2. _____
3. _____

Foster Your Interdependence

1. _____
2. _____
3. _____

Be Yourself

1. _____
2. _____
3. _____

BE VULNERABLE

*One of the most important traits for today's leader is to
be vulnerable.*

—Tom Chappell,
founder, Tom's of Maine

IT USED TO be that the boss was expected to know it all. At the turn
of the last century, business was relatively simple. A person took a craft,
became good at it, sold his or her product, and expanded the business.
As the business grew the owner, or "boss," led the enterprise by mastering what was required to go to the next level. There was little specialization. So as the business grew, the boss pretty much did know it all.
Now business is much more complex. Increased competition, the technology revolution, innovative financing schemes, complex personnel issues, and sophisticated marketing approaches have created a universe of
specialists.

In most cases these specialists are a whole lot smarter at their part of
the business than the boss. No longer the smartest of the bunch, the
CEO creates the environment, establishes the ground rules, and molds
people of differing disciplines, attitudes, and values into a powerful
whole. Max DePree, former CEO of Herman Miller, puts it this way:
"The first responsibility of a leader is to define reality. The last is to say
thank you."[4]

Perhaps this is why EQ (Emotional Quotient) received so much attention. IQ (Intelligence Quotient) is a measure of intellect; EQ is the
measure of "street smarts" and ability to relate to and work effectively
with people. In his book, *Working with Emotional Intelligence*, Daniel
Goleman reports that for an entry-level person EQ is twice as important as IQ or competencies as a performance indicator. As a person is

promoted to higher positions in the organization, EQ takes on increasing weight, until at the CEO level it accounts for 90 percent of a leader's effectiveness. If you think of IQ as relating to a particular discipline like technology or marketing, and EQ as relating to managing people and creating effective teams of high powered "experts," the shift toward EQ is logical.

Like Tom Chappell, founding chairman of Tom's of Maine, today's effective leader knows that he or she does not have all the answers and has to rely on others for them. In this context the phrase, "I don't know"—words that might have shaken the confidence of an entire organization in the past—must become a part of the head person's parlance. At a strategy meeting with his executive team, Bob Galvin, the son of Paul Galvin, the founder of Motorola, confessed that he didn't know enough to make Motorola competitive. In a moment of vulnerability, here was the founder's son telling his team that he didn't know how to extend this great company's past success into the future.

What was the result of this extraordinary admission? First, the executives marshaled the resources required to create a rock-solid strategy for future success. But even more important, Galvin's admission gave every Motorola employee permission to show his or her own vulnerability and openly inform managers when he or she didn't know enough. Instead of punishing employees for knowledge gaps, Motorola placed major emphasis on the development of its people. Today, they spend more on per-employee training than almost any other company in the country. Galvin's simple act of vulnerability created a legacy of honesty and personal growth that flourishes to this day.

Another form of vulnerability is to show emotions, something that the tough and hardened leader was long forbidden to do. A *20/20* profile of John Chambers, CEO of Cisco Systems, demonstrates how far corporate culture has shifted. During the interview, Chambers discussed the pain and anguish of having to lay off 5,000 people at a previous company, and as he recalled the situation, his eyes welled with tears. Do we think less of him or view him as weak? Of course not. Rather, we appreciate his genuine concern for the working person and, for many of us, secretly wish we had the opportunity to work for such an extraordinary human being. Compassion is not just acceptable, it's essential to successful leadership.

If your intent is to embrace and be an example of one or more of the Six Ways of Being, your willingness to be vulnerable will become an ally. No doubt you are more comfortable and accomplished in some of the ways than others. It is in the areas that you have the most room for growth that you are most likely to stumble and perhaps even embarrass yourself. This is precisely when vulnerability—admitting you don't know and giving yourself credit for trying—will help keep you on the path you have chosen. Your intent and willingness to try new models will ultimately get you and your team to where you want to be.

BE A CHEERLEADER

Invite people to delight in their own genius.

—ANTON ARMBRUSTER,
consultant

IN THE LATE 1980s and early 1990s the quality movement took United States industry by storm. Following the storied success of Japanese companies that reinvented themselves after World War II, American executives formed quality departments and sought the newly created national quality prize, the Malcolm Baldrige National Quality Award. Unbeknown to many of these leaders, the changes required to introduce the tenets and practices of total quality would, in fact, require an entirely new work culture.

During this time, the Forum Corporation sponsored a meeting of quality officers from a number of companies that were successfully leading the quality charge. Almost every quality officer reported that the

Use Your Strengths

Identify one of the Six Ways of Being you feel most confident with. List three ways you can use this strength to help you create a powerful working environment for your team.

1. _____

2. _____

3. _____

Identify Your Challenges

Identify which one of the Six Ways of Being will be most challenging for you to adopt.

- What are three actions you can take to make this way second nature to you?

  1. _____

  2. _____

  3. _____

- How will you handle slipups when trying to internalize this way of being?

- Who on your team has mastered this way of being and how can you secure his or her help as you try to master it yourself?

most important action a CEO could take to successfully instill quality thinking and procedures was to become a cheerleader, and conspicuously support all people and activities that moved the company toward total quality. It wasn't about funding. It wasn't about strategy. It wasn't about public statements. It was about showing up and recognizing people at all levels in the organization who were making a sincere effort to change their company by changing themselves.

Being recognized is one of our core needs, and recognition becomes increasingly important when we are undertaking a task or project that will force us out of our comfort zone. During those first tentative steps into uncharted territory, it is so important to acknowledge the effort of trying to change and to celebrate those "early wins" it produces. One well-timed word of encouragement at these tenuous moments can have a huge impact on the chances for success. When you recognize the efforts of your team as they adopt new values, you reinforce their risk taking and create new energy as they work toward their goals.

Catch Someone Doing Something Right

> *You must awaken values, awaken your people's remembrance of their power to create and call your people to their best.*
>
> —Wind Eagle and Rainbow Hawk,
> *cofounders, Ehama Institute*

TO MOTIVATE YOUR team, make it part of your daily practice to notice and comment on the changes made by at least three people. Use specific comments to show that you are observing their efforts and appreciate them. For instance, when you offer such motivational feedback as, "I noticed that you were hesitant to share your opinion during the meeting and I want to acknowledge you for offering your expertise," you lock in those positive steps for the future. The more specific your comments, the more powerful the incentive to incorporate that particular behavior on a daily basis.

Focusing on motivational feedback is essential to counterbalance the natural tendency most performers have to dwell on their shortcomings. Putting your primary accent on what *is* working is critical to keeping spirits high and energized.

How Bad Do People Feel about Mistakes?

MOST PEOPLE ARE harder on themselves than we will ever be. Remember the Inner Critic? They see and feel bad about their mistakes as soon as they happen. Having a manager come in and comment on what they already know adds no new knowledge and only makes them feel worse. Try this experiment:

1. Ask the person to critique his or her own performance.
2. Notice their ratio of positive to negative comments. Indeed, does he or she even comment on what went well?
3. If he or she left out a critical — and I mean critical — mistake, you can point it out.
4. Comment on at least three positive aspects of the person's performance. Be specific.

Clarifying Your Values

BEING A LEADER is a little like walking in the snow — you leave tracks that are quite visible. Whether we like it or not, anyone who works for or around us and cares to notice our tracks can tell a great deal about us. Perhaps the most telltale signs will be about what we truly value. In spite of what we say, do we really care about developing people? Do we really want to exceed our customers' expectations? Do we really want to invest in long-term projects? Do we really speak our truth? Do we really operate with integrity?

Are You Living Your Values?

- Typical values might include, but are certainly not limited to, achievement, fame, friendship, health, personal growth, power, recognition, wealth, wisdom, etc. Take a moment and on separate Post-it notes write each of the core values that are most important to you as a businessperson. Now place all of the values you have listed in a column. From the column pick your five most important values and arrange them in order of importance, from top to bottom.

- Separate the top five and ask yourself, "Are these really my top five values?" If not, replace those that aren't with others that are. Now test each of your top five values by honestly assessing whether your behaviors are actually consistent with the value in question. Be brutally honest, because others see clearly what you value through your behavior. For example, one executive stated that "work-family balance" was an important core value but he worked seventy hours a week and routinely spent a good part of most Saturdays and Sundays in the office. Another executive included "health" in his top five yet was thirty pounds overweight, smoked heavily, and didn't exercise. He was thinking of his idealized values rather than what was actually reflected in his behavior.

- Are any of your values inconsistent with your desire to bring the Six Ways of Being alive in your work group? If so, how will you resolve this conflict? Which values will help?

Living by Values

CHARLIE EITEL, THE CEO of the Simmons Mattress Company, is known for turning around a number of struggling companies during his career. Unlike the legendary "Hacksaw" Reynolds, who made his name with wholesale firings in the companies he was called to rescue, Charlie takes a different approach. He creates purpose, values, and priorities and then reinforces them rigorously. Some staff leave the company, but a core group commits to both the new company values and development plans to improve their performance.

Charlie says, "I want to create an environment where people will want

to stay." He does this with a simple five-point leadership approach that
has been the cornerstone of his success:

1. Pick good people.
2. Help them create their own vision.
3. Help them set priorities.
4. Support them (let go).
5. Help them achieve their own greatness.

This is a remarkably simple approach that is totally centered around
the well-being and support of the employee. No wonder people want to
work for Charlie. And the oil that keeps these five actions working
smoothly? Clear, specific, public, and incessant cheerleading.

Perhaps the best executive cheerleader I have ever met is Edson
Bueno, founder and CEO of Assistencia Medica International (Amil),
a major health care provider in Brazil. During a day with him at his
offices in São Paulo, not one person escaped his positive feedback. In
the halls, in the elevator, in the dining room, in the parking lot, and
yes, even in the men's room, he was a walking bundle of enthusiastic
compliments that bordered on adulation for his employees. He knew
every employee and would unfailingly relate some unique aspect of the
person's professional or private life to me. All the people responded with
pride in themselves and their work. Is it any wonder that Amil is one
of the fastest growing and most profitable companies in Latin America?

What Will Your Leadership Legacy Be?

THIS IS THE last, and for you, the leader, perhaps the most important
exercise in this book. I encourage you to give it your thoughtful attention. Earlier we talked about the tracks you leave as a leader. Taken
together, these tracks form what could be called your legacy. Most leaders are so focused on handling today's pressures that they haven't really
considered the kind of leadership legacy they want to leave behind. They

get caught in the trap of expediency and miss the opportunity to create a powerful and enduring positive legacy.

Consider this: You are already creating your legacy as a leader—the question is, are you intentional about how you are creating it? If I asked those people you manage what they think of you as a leader, what would you want them to say? How does this compare with what they would actually say? You have a choice here. Are you exercising it?

- On a piece of paper write what you want your legacy to be. Start with, "My legacy as a leader will be that, above all else, . . .

  _____

  _____

  _____ "

- Try to limit your list of legacy results to no more than five. Too many will cause you to lose focus.

Cindi Love, chairperson of Integration Control Systems & Services, Inc., a consulting firm in Abilene, Texas, understands the idea of a positive leadership legacy. Her note to ICSS employees may inspire you as you begin to shape a workplace where you, and each and every one of your employees, love the work you're with:

There is a place in every person's heart that I believe is Higher Ground—a place where even in the worst of times, the person is his or her best self— unselfish, forgiving, listening, encouraging, serving, caring, just, honest, clear-thinking. Within the group of people we call ICSS, the best self is often a visitor—you are true servants of your fellow man—in your actions, thoughts, and deeds. For that I am grateful and I want you to know that I am proud of you and humbled to be your leader. Thank you for the wonderful work that you do with our customers and with each other.

Leadership must adapt itself to the changing needs of customers, their industry, the economy—as well as those they are leading. It's a tall order. They need to be able to withstand the vicissitudes of a new generation with differing values, the virtual organizations, rampant technology, staggering short-term demands, global reach, volatile economies, escalating job requirements, new competency requirements, and customers who expect an instant response. The old leadership paradigms simply no longer work. What is required today is an organic approach, one that can reflexively adapt to the changing circumstances of the people being led. The one-size-fits-all, static-leadership model lacks the flexibility to retain any semblance of effectiveness. While the Six Ways of Being are not all-inclusive, they do offer a new approach for thinking about your task as a leader. Whether your intention is to bring them fully to life in your organization or simply accent them within the bounds of established values, your efforts will be greatly enhanced by your willingness and ability to *live the Six Ways, be vulnerable, and be a cheerleader.* If this is a path you have chosen in part or in entirety, I wish you good luck.

Action Steps

BASED ON THE information and exercises in this chapter I will do the following:

- I will start . . .

- I will stop . . .

- I will do more . . .

- I will do less . . .

- I will do differently . . .

How Good a Leader Are You?: Self-Assessment

INSTRUCTIONS:

Using a 1-to-5 scale, assign a rating to each practice that best describes the extent to which you engage in it.

1 = Never
3 = Sometimes
5 = Always

For best results, be totally candid. If you are undecided between two numbers select the lower one. Because we usually know the "right" answer and think we are doing the "right" things, try to rate this self-assessment as the people you lead would rate you. A good test is to ask, "If my team saw how I rated myself, would they agree?"

YOUR RATING PRACTICE

1. ___ I thoroughly understand the motivation of every person who reports to me.

2. ___ My work units have a clear vision that is understood by all.

3. ___ I give more recognition than criticism.

4. ___ I have no problem admitting my mistakes to others.

5. ___ My work unit has a clear set of values that are understood by all.

6. ___ I am willing to dismiss any person who is unwilling to live by our values.

7. ___ I have great passion for my work.

8. ___ I tell the truth to my people.

9. ___ I have a strong network of people I connect with at work.

10. ___ I am able to laugh at my own mistakes.

11. ___ I listen to understand rather than to answer.

12. ___ Even when there is risk to me, I am willing to take a stand for what is important to my team.

___ Total Score

INTERPRETATION:

Place your total score (total of all twelve ratings) on the following scale to gain some insights and suggestions about your self-assessment.

12–21	It appears that you are not engaging in a number of the practices that can enhance your effectiveness as a leader. Ask yourself why. What can you do to improve? Who can help you by providing objective feedback?
22–29	Although there appears to be some strengths in your use of the practices, your overall score is relatively low. Explore why this may be and determine what you can do to

	use these practices to enhance your effectiveness as a leader. Who can help you?
30–38	This score represents modest use of the leadership practices. Continue doing what you do well and plan to improve those practices where your rating was low.
39–47	You appear to have strength in utilizing the twelve leadership practices. Keep doing what you do well and determine what you can do to strengthen the practices you rated as low.
48–56	Congratulations. You appear to be utilizing the leadership practices extensively. Keep it up and fine-tune your approach by determining where you can improve and then initiate such improvements.

Note: This questionnaire has not been validated through rigorous research. It is intended to stimulate you to ask critical questions that will enhance your effectiveness as a leader.

Notes

WELCOME

1 Clay Siegert, "Concession King Lands Sales Job," *Boston Herald*, August 31, 1998.

1. FOLLOW YOUR PASSION

1 Harriet Rubin, "Art of Darkness," *Fast Company*, October 1998.

2 Maria Atanasov, "Interview: A Billion or Bust," *Your Company*, October 1, 1998.

3 Tom McNichol, "Daddy Starbucks," *USA Weekend*, September 7, 1997.

4 Pamela Ferdinand, "In R. I., Doing the Traffic Jam," *The Washington Post*, December 24, 1999; Julie Goodman, "R. I. Dancing Cop Entertains Drivers," Associated Press, December 24, 1999; Todd Bensman, "Speedway's Owner, Dancing Cop Move Fast to Smooth Traffic Woes," *The Dallas Morning News*, April 6, 1997.

5 Peter B. Vaill, "Executive Development as Spiritual Development," in Suresh Srivasta, David L. Cooperrider, et al., eds., *Appreciative Management and Leadership*, rev. ed. (Jossey-Bass, 1990). See also his "The Requisites of Visionary Leadership" in *Managing as a Performing Art* (Jossey-Bass, 1989).

6 William C. Taylor, "Inspired by Work," *Fast Company*, November 1999.

7 Per individual investor/financial analyst Eileen Levi, who researched stock information for the book.

8 American Medical Association Council on Long Range Planning and Development, Report A: "Physician and Public Attitudes on Medicine as a

Career" (Policy No. H-405.984), December 1989, reaffirmed in the "Sunset Report," June 2000.

9 Susan Trausch, "Career Peak: Bottom Rung," *The Boston Globe*, February 6, 2000.

10 Alan M. Webber, "Are You Deciding on Purpose," *Fast Company*, February–March 1998.

11 Charles Eitel, *Eitel Time: Turnaround Secrets* (Harcourt Brace, 1995).

2. BE HOME

1 Quoted in "Searching for the Soul," *Life*, December 1997.

2 Ibid.

3 Thomas Jefferson to Francis Eppes, 1816, *The Writings of Thomas Jefferson* (Memorial Edition), Andrew Lipscomb and Albert E. Bergh, eds. (Thomas Jefferson Memorial Association of the United States, 1903–1919), p. 242.

4 Hugh Prather, *Notes to Myself* (Bantam Books, 1983).

5 Marilyn Wellemeyer, "On Your Own Time: Sports Schools Go High Tech," *Fortune*, February 16, 1987.

6 Greg Gutfeld, "Head Coaching," *Men's Health*, November 1, 1995.

7 "The Angry Vital Center," *The New Democrat*, November 1994.

8 John Skow, "The Fairway Less Traveled," *Time*, September 19, 1994.

9 Quoted in Robert A. Mamis, "Black-Belt Boss," *Inc.*, September 1, 1996.

10 Paul Choi and Shawn Hutchinson, "Quick Guide to Meditation," Duke Meditation Group, http://www.duke.edu/web/meditation/quickguide.html, April 1, 1998.

11 Polly LaBarre, "The Agenda — Grassroots Leadership," *Fast Company*, April 1999.

12 David C. McClelland, *Human Motivation* (Cambridge University Press, 1998).

13 John Jeansonne, "Nagano 1998/Gold at End of Rainbow," *Newsday*, February 21, 1998.

14 Adam Rogers, "Zen and the Art of Olympic Success," *Newsweek*, July 22, 1996.

3. CREATE YOUR OWN REALITY

1 Hugh Prather, *Notes to Myself* (Bantam Books, 1983).

2 *60 Minutes* transcript, "The Mother of Invention," March 29, 1998.

3 Jim Sigmon, "Opening Doors to the Web," *The Dallas Morning News*, April 6, 2000.

4 Al Siebert, "When *How* You React Makes a Difference" (Practical Psychology Press, 1997).

5 John Stossel, "The Mystery of Happiness," ABC Special Report, September 4, 1997.

6 Dan Seligman, "Does Money Buy Happiness?," *Forbes*, April 21, 1997.

7 Rae Corelli, "Get Happy!: Experts Debate Whether the Key to Happiness Lies in the Genes," *Maclean's*, September 16, 1996, which cites the article, "Who Is Happy?," by David G. Myers and Ed Diener in the May 1996 edition of *Psychological Science* describing their original research.

8 Ed Diener and David G. Myers, "The Science of Happiness," *The Futurist*, September–October 1997.

9 Myers and Diener, "The Science of Happiness."

10 Mary Harris, "Be Happy, Live Longer," ABCnews.com, February 8, 2000.

11 Adam Khan, "Optimists Are Back at Work Faster after Job Loss," *Detroit Free Press*, January 7, 1997.

12 Francie Baltazar-Schwartz, "Attitude Is Everything," in Jack Canfield (ed.), *Chicken Soup for the Soul at Work: 101 Stories of Courage, Compassion, and Creativity in the Workplace* (Health Communications, 1996).

13 Michael Scheier and Charles Carver, "The Life Orientation Test," *Journal of Personality and Social Psychology* 67(1994).

14 Terence Monmaney, "Brighter Vision," *Newsday*, February 5, 2000.

15 Khan, "Optimists Are Back at Work Faster after Job Loss."

16 Ibid.

17 Michelle Neely Martinez, "The Smarts That Count," *HR*, November 1997.

18 Alan Farnham, "Are You Smart Enough to Keep Your Job?" *Fortune*, January 15, 1996.

19 Stossel, "Mystery of Happiness."

20 Corelli, "Get Happy!"

21 From a speech given on accepting the Entrepreneur of the Year Award sponsored by the National Foundation of Women Business Owners, at the National Press Club in Washington, D.C., April 7, 2000.

4. GET OUT OF YOUR OWN WAY

1 Pamela Kruger, "A Leader's Journey," *Fast Company*, June 1999.

2 Ibid.

3 Sally Jenkins, "Point After: They Came to the French Open Playing on Their Memories," *Sports Illustrated*, June 8, 1992.

4 Anne B. Fisher, "Are You Afraid of Success?" *Fortune*, July 8, 1996.

5 Quoted in Ann Reeves, "Time Management: Understanding the Role of Failure," *The Pacific Coast Business Times*, July 1998.

6 Quoted in "The Quotable Entrepreneur," *Inc.*, May 2000.

7 Fisher, "Are You Afraid of Success?"

8 Ibid.

9 Theodore Roosevelt, *History as Literature* (Charles Scribner's Sons, 1913).

10 Marianne Williamson, *A Return to Love: Reflections on the Principles of a Course in Miracles*, (HarperCollins, 1996).

5. FOSTER YOUR INTERDEPENDENCE

1 Quoted in John A. Byrne, "The Global Corporation Becomes the Leaderless Corporation," *Business Week*, August 30, 1999.

2 Michelle Conlin, "Religion in the Workplace," *Business Week*, November 1, 1999.

3 Ian I. Mitroff and Elizabeth A. Denton, "A Study of Spirituality in the Workplace," *Sloan Management Review*, June 22, 1999.

4 Michael Kaplan, "How to Overcome Your Strengths," *Fast Company*, May 1999.

5 Ibid.

6 1999 Emerging Workforce Study, by Spherion Corporation, in conjunction with Louis Harris and Associates, Inc.

7 George H. Litwin and Robert A. Stringer, Jr., *Motivation and Organizational Climate* (Harvard University, 1968).

8 Personal conversation with Donald Tosti. See also Donald Tosti and Stephanie Jackson, "Feedback," in H. Stolovitch and E. Keeps (eds.), *Handbook of Human Performance Technology* (Jossey-Bass, 1999).

6. BE YOURSELF

1 Betsy Morris, "The Brand's the Thing," *Fortune*, March 4, 1996.

2 Gus Blanchard, "Diversity in the Workplace Makes Good Business Sense: Companies Benefit When They Leverage the Talents of All Potential Members of the Work Force," *Minneapolis Star Tribune*, October 26, 1998, citing *The Wall Street Journal* of May 4, 1993.

3 Sidney (Shuichi) Yoshida, "Quality Improvement and TQC Management at Calsonic in Japan and Overseas," paper prepared for the Second International Quality Symposium in Mexico, November 1989.

4 Michelle Conlin, "The Truth," *Forbes*, February 10, 1997.

5 Fred Andrews, "Hard Lessons Learned at Schwab," *The New York Times*, April 30, 2000.

6 Carol Hymowitz, "Wasted Skills: Bosses Often Overlook a Big Talent Pool— Their Staffs," *Chicago Tribune*, May 28, 2000.

7 "Unit of One Anniversary Handbook," *Fast Company*, February 1997.

7. LEADER'S GUIDE: HOW TO CREATE A SPIRITED WORKFORCE

1 Alan G. Robinson and Sam Stern, *Corporate Creativity: How Innovation and Improvement Actually Happen* (Berrett-Koelher, 1997).

2 John P. Kotter and James L. Heskett, *Corporate Culture and Performance* (Free Press, 1992).

3 Anne Fisher, "The World's Most Admired Companies," *Fortune*, October 27, 1997.

4 Max DePree, *Leadership Is an Act* (Doubleday Books, 1989).

Bibliography

1. FOLLOW YOUR PASSION

Collins, James C., and Jerry I. Porras. *Built to Last: Successful Habits of Visionary Companies.* HarperCollins, 1994.

Edler, Richard. *If I Knew Then What I Know Now: CEO's and Other Smart Executives Share Wisdom They Wish They'd Been Told 25 Years Ago.* Berkley Publishing Group, 1997 (reprint edition).

Eitel, Charles. *Eitel Time: Turnaround Secrets.* Harcourt Brace, 1995.

George, Judy, and Todd Lyon. *Intuitive Businesswoman.* Clarkson Potter, 2000.

Leider, Richard. *The Power of Purpose.* MJF Books, 2000.

Schultz, Howard, and Dori Jones Yang. *Pour Your Heart into It: How Starbucks Built a Company One Cup at a Time.* Hyperion, 1997.

2. BE HOME

Chopra, Deepak. *The Seven Spiritual Laws of Success: A Practical Guide to the Fulfillment of Your Dreams.* Amber-Allen Publishing, 1995.

Kabat-Zinn, Jon. *Wherever You Go, There You Are: Mindful Meditation in Everyday Life.* Hyperion, 1995.

Kaplan, Robert S., and David P. Norton. *The Balanced Scorecard: Translating Strategy into Action.* Harvard Business School Press, 1996.

Land, George, and Beth Jarman. *Breakpoint and Beyond: Mastering the Future Today.* Leadership 2000 Inc., 1998.

McCluggage, Denise. *The Centered Skier*. Tempest Book Shop, 1999.

Prather, Hugh. *Notes to Myself*. Bantam Books, 1983 (reissue edition).

3. CREATE YOUR OWN REALITY

Glasser, William. *Reality Therapy: A New Approach to Psychiatry*. Harper-Collins, 1989.

Jaworski, Joe. *Synchronicity: The Inner Path of Leadership*, Betty Sue Flowers (ed.) Berrett-Koehler, 1998.

Scheier, Michael, and Charles S. Carver. *Perspectives on Personality*. Allyn & Bacon, 1999.

Seligman, Martin E. P. *Learned Optimism: How to Change Your Mind and Your Life*. Pocket Books, 1998.

Siebert, Al, and Bernie S. Siegel. *The Survivor Personality: Why Some People are Stronger, Smarter, and More Skillful at Handling Life's Difficulties . . . and How You Can Be, Too*. Berkley Publishing Group, 1996.

Vaughan, Susan. *Half Empty, Half Full: Understanding the Psychological Roots of Optimism*. Harcourt Brace, 2000.

Zukav, Gary. *The Seat of the Soul*. Fireside, 1990.

4. GET OUT OF YOUR OWN WAY

Arrien, Angeles. *The Four-Fold Way: Walking the Paths of the Warrior, Teacher, Healer and Visionary*. Harper San Francisco, 1993.

Bach, Richard. *The Bridge across Forever*. Dell Books, 1986 (reissue edition).

———. *Illusions: The Adventures of a Reluctant Messiah*. Dell Publishing Company, 1998.

Stone, Hal, and Sidra Stone *Embracing Your Inner Critic: Turning Self-Criticism into a Creative Asset*. Harper San Francisco, 1993.

5. FOSTER YOUR INTERDEPENDENCE

Buckingham, Marcus, and Curt Coffman. *First, Break all the Rules: What the World's Greatest Managers Do Differently*. Simon and Schuster, 1999.

Clarke, Jane. *Office Politics: A Survival Guide*. Industrial Society, 1999.

Frankel, Lois P. *Jump-Start Your Career: How the "Strengths" That Got You Where You Are Today Can Hold You Back Tomorrow.* Three Rivers Press, 1998.

McClelland, David C. *Human Motivation.* Cambridge University Press, 1998 (reprint edition).

McLagan, Patricia. *On the Level: Performance Communication That Works.* Berrett-Koehler, 1995.

Mitroff, Ian, and Elizabeth Denton. *A Spiritual Audit of Corporate America: A Hard Look at Spirituality, Religion, and Values in the Workplace* (Jossey-Bass Business & Management Series). Jossey-Bass, 1999.

Naisbitt, John, Nana Naisbitt, and Douglas Philips. *High Tech, High Touch: Technology and Our Search for Meaning.* Broadway Books, 1999.

Senge, Peter. *The Fifth Discipline: The Art and Practice of the Learning Organization.* Currency/Doubleday, 1994.

Wieder, Marcia. *Making Your Dreams Come True.* Harmony Books, 1999.

Zander, Rosamund, and Benjamin Zander. *The Art of Possibility.* Harvard Business School Press, 2000.

6. BE YOURSELF

Bohm, David. *On Dialogue.* Routledge, 1996.

Cousins, Norman. *Anatomy of an Illness as Perceived by the Patient.* Bantam, Doubleday, Dell Publishing, 1991.

Freiberg, Kevin, and Jackie Freiberg. *Nuts: Southwest Airlines' Crazy Recipe for Business and Personal Success.* Bard Press, 1996.

Gallwey, W. Timothy, Robert Kriegel, and Bob Kriegel. *Inner Skiing.* Random House, 1997.

Kataria, Madan. *Laugh for No Reason.* Madhuri International, 1999.

Pottruck, David, and David Pearce. *Clicks and Mortar.* Jossey-Bass, 2000.

Whiteley, Richard, and Diane Hessan. *Customer Centered Growth: Five Proven Strategies for Building Competitive Advantage.* Perseus, 1997.

7. LEADER'S GUIDE: HOW TO CREATE A SPIRITED WORKFORCE

Goleman, Daniel. *Working with Emotional Intelligence*. Bantam Books, 1998.

Goss, Tracy, and Betty Sue Flowers. *The Last Word on Power: Reinvention for Leaders and Anyone Who Must Make the Impossible Happen*. Currency/ Doubleday, 1995.

Pfeffer, Jeffery, and Robert I. Sutton. *The Knowing-Doing Gap: How Smart Companies Turn Knowledge into Action*. Harvard Business School Press, 2000.

Acknowledgments

I have often been asked how long it took me to write *Love the Work You're With* and found it to be a rather difficult question. The short answer is about two years. But the more accurate answer is a lifetime. *Love the Work You're With* represents a lifetime of personal experience that has been distilled into the Six Ways of Being. Because of this I am indebted to the many people who have entered my life as formal or informal teachers. Each and every one of them has contributed in some way to what has been written and it is to them that this book is dedicated.

To those leaders who have and will create the kinds of working environments that support the Six Ways of Being, I offer thanks and deep gratitude. These are the leaders who "get it" about people and are willing to invest in the human resource even in the face of unmerciful pressure to achieve short-term earnings. Among them are: Dr. Edson Bueno, CEO, Amil Healthcare Systems; John Chambers, CEO, Cisco Systems; Tom Chappell, CEO, Tom's of Maine; Robbie Delgado, CEO, NWT Philippines; Charlie Eitel, CEO, Simmons Mattress; Carly Fiorina, CEO, Hewlett-Packard; Judy George, CEO, Domain; Bob Galvin, former CEO, Motorola; Herb Kelleher, CEO, Southwest Airlines; Sir Colin Marshall, former CEO, British Airways; Julian Richer, CEO, Richer Sounds; and Anita Roddick, CEO, The Body Shop. These leaders, and others like them, are proof positive that "nice people can finish first."

Direct contributors to the book who provided us with helpful interviews and/or insights include: Jim Anastasi, Richard Atlas, Curt Berrien, Ted Berman, Joanne Brem, Betty Sue Flowers, Mardi Gardner, Ric Giardina, Fred Jordan, Max McCormick, Steven Meyer, Pamela Oesterlin, Phillip Rubin, Mary Beth Shoening, Linda Stone, Hal and Sidra Stone, and Marilyn Thomas.

When *Love the Work You're With* was first conceived, I asked any of Forum's professionals and associates to contact me if they were interested in helping with the book. The response was overwhelming as more than forty people responded. They included: Louise Aaxon, Anton Armbruster, Chuck Becker, Susan Beckman, Curt Berrien, Ed Boswell, Linda Brainan, Jennifer Potter Brotman, Sarene Byrne, Jane Carroll, David Carter, Roxanne Darling, Marlene Dolan, Paul Dredge, Barry Freeman, Jane Harris, John Humphrey, Galina Jeffrey, Gregg Johnson, Kerry Johnson, George Johnstone, Gerald Jones, Nancy Lague, Molly Maginn, Jeff Meleski, Anne O'Brien, Ellen Ponder, Emarie Pope, Sarah Risher, Jonathan Rosin, Jane Saltonstall, Shaum Smith, Sally Sparhawk, Marion Their, Maribeth Wahle, Joe Wheeler, and Bill Woolfolk.

Special insights, encouragement, and hard work were graciously offered throughout the entire project by Maria Broderick, Roxanne Darling, Christie Jacobs, Pat McClagan, and Shala Roberts. Whenever I felt stuck they seemed to have the ability to jump-start the creative process once again. Laura Mather, my assistant while at Forum, was both encouraging and responsive to the numerous administrative and clerical demands of such an undertaking.

David Sobel of Henry Holt had a vision for *Love the Work You're With* that combined the "soft" aspects of creating passion for one's work with the practicality of "hard" how-to's from organizational life. He never wavered from this vision and helped us create a book that we hope balances these two realms in a practical and helpful manner. Holt's Robin Dennis is a superb editor. Her uncanny ability to trim prosaic fat, reorder concepts, and suggest new approaches greatly enriched the book.

Jan Miller of Dupree, Miller and Associates is a literary agent of the first order. She knows book writing and publishing inside out and is an astute businessperson who has the vision for what's possible. In every interaction with her and her staff, I always felt I was unquestionably in the hands of competent professionals.

Annie Post is a wonderful writer and even more wonderful colleague. We have collaborated on three books and established a partnership I value greatly. She takes my preliminary concepts and writing and enriches them with poignant anecdotes and validating research. In addition, she models what this book is about and with the loving support of her children dedicates whatever time is required to get the job done.

In my world of writing, no one stands taller than my brother, Peter Hillyer. For a third time he has transformed helpful prose into a light, fast-moving rendering of important material. Peter waves his literary wand and the books we produce positively sparkle.

Sharon Whiteley is my wife and best friend. She is also an astute, award-winning entrepreneur whose helpful critique of my work kept it grounded in the everyday business realities most of us face.

Index

reality testing, 118
reason for being, 34, 36
recognition, 3, 220–22
"Rediscovering the Artist Within"
 (workshop), 139
reengineer your job, 5, 20, 39–47,
 131
resilience, 90, 91, 107–8
resources
 and mistakes, 131, 132
 underdeveloped, 145, 147
respect, 199
 for employees, 18
results, 71, 72, 82
 emphasis on, 72, 73f
 and expectations, 77–78
 fixation on, 80–81
 goals and, 72–73
reward yourself, 103
rewards
 intangible, 199
 internal/external, 25
Reynolds, "Hacksaw," 223
rhythm, 23
Robertson, Frederick W., 83
roles
 and genius, 139, 141, 143
Roosevelt, Franklin Delano, 86
Roosevelt, Theodore, 144
root, ability to, 52, 53
Rubin, Phillip, 146
rules
 and genius, 139–41

S

salary, 75
sales quota(s), 81–83
Saturn Corporation, 210
Scandinavian Designs, 15
Schachter-Shalomi, Zalman, 49
Scheier, Michael, 93

Schoening, Mary Beth, 160
Schrager, Ian, 100
Schultz, Howard, 17–18, 19, 23
Schulze, Richard, 186
Schwartz, Brian, 139
self talk, 117, 123
 monitoring, 125
self-acceptance, 185
self-assessment
 leadership, 227–29
self-assessment questionnaire, 8,
 9–13
self-care, 200–203
self-compassion, 207
self-esteem, 102, 113, 119
 and happiness, 90
 healthy body image in, 105
self-love, 205–7
self-mastery
 power of, 109–10
self-recrimination, 96
self-respect, 202
self-sabotage, 116, 128
 on the job, 117
 motivation and, 117–18
self-worth, 71
Seligman, Martin E. P., 95
Senge, Peter
 Fifth Discipline, The, 167
Sheppard-Missett, Judi, 105
Simmons Mattress Company, 223
Six Ways of Being, 5–6, 7–8, 185,
 208, 226
 bringing into work unit, 211–12
 interpreting, 13
 living, 213–16
 reinforcing, 215
skills, 3, 27, 29, 30
 and mistakes, 131
skills development, 168, 169
Sloan Management Review, 153

RICHARD C. WHITELEY is the author of the award-winning bestsellers, *The Customer-Driven Company* (Addison-Wesley, 1991) and *Customer-Centered Growth* (Addison-Wesley, 1996). A successful businessman, he is principal of The Whiteley Group, an international speaking and consulting firm. Previously, he held the position of vice chairman of the Forum Corporation, a 700-person global training firm he cofounded in 1971. As a leading author and speaker on customer service, leadership, and respiriting work, he has worked with more than 300 companies in twenty-six countries and is a frequent speaker at major industry conventions and leading colleges and universities. He received his MBA from Harvard Business School and resides in Boston, Massachusetts, with his wife, Sharon.